T0322272

ROBERT SHEEHAN

Playing Dead

HOW MEDITATION BROUGHT ME BACK TO LIFE

RIDER

4

Rider, an imprint of Ebury Publishing
20 Vauxhall Bridge Road
London SW1V 2SA

Rider is part of the Penguin Random House group of companies whose
addresses can be found at global.penguinrandomhouse.com

Penguin
Random House
UK

First published by Rider in 2024

www.penguin.co.uk

A CIP catalogue record for this book is available from the British Library

ISBN 9781846047350

Designed by Seagull Design

Typeset in 11/15.9 pt Electra LT Std by Jouve (UK), Milton Keynes
Printed and bound in Great Britain by Clays Ltd, Elcograf S.p.A.

The authorised representative in the EEA is Penguin Random House Ireland,
Morrison Chambers, 32 Nassau Street, Dublin D02 YH68

Penguin Random House is committed to a sustainable future for
our business, our readers and our planet. This book is made
from Forest Stewardship Council® certified paper.

To Augustina

Contents

Preface

After about a year of struggle, the simple practice of meditation began transporting me to parts of myself that I'd never been to before. It taught me how to reveal, layer by layer, the things that were going on in my subconscious awareness, so that they could also become part of my conscious awareness.

The purpose of this book is not to set myself up as an expert in the practice of meditation, but only to confirm the opposite: that I am a complete beginner of meditation, writing from what the great engineer and meditator Itzhak Bentov called 'my present level of ignorance'. I am no expert in human behaviour, I'm just someone who was compelled to find a practice – one that is laughably simple – to be profoundly life-changing.

By this stage, I have been practising the art of sitting still over many thousands of hours for about seven years now. But if it were an evening's chat down the pub, it still feels like I'd be only just after clearing my throat.

In that time, the practice has yielded a profound transformation. It has allowed me to retrieve my real self, below/above/ beyond my day-to-day impulse-driven self (after years spent pretending other ones).

It has proven to me that one does not need fancy credentials or to have climbed a dangerous mountain to begin expanding their consciousness and experiencing more joyful spaciousness, and has permitted me to see with greater clarity behind the curtain of this strange and wonderful thing we call being alive as a human being.

You'll have already noticed how, when I refer directly to what this book is about, the word(s) symbolising it will be in the process of dissolving. I persisted in using completely blank spaces originally where the word meditation would be, but the blank spaces were tripping up people's reading rhythm.

A dissolving word or phrase is a more accurate symbol than a blank space on the page anyhow. Because one cannot just leap from the state of consciousness required to be reading, to a state of complete blanknessness, and then back again in a split second. It takes time to travel from one space to the other.

I symbolise it on the page this way because I've found that using any word to name it is inappropriate. Meditation is a wordless place. Words that have been traditionally used to name the practice have too many cobwebs attached to them. Savouring the taste of being is just like food: it cannot be tasted by reading the menu.

So as to avoid being vague about it, I define meditation as a wordless, action-less pastime which, when awarded your valuable time, space and attention, greatly unfolds in dimension.

It is a state in which I sit/lay quiet(ish) and still(ish), where I am left entirely to my own devices, not speaking or doing anything. All the while accepting wholeheartedly everything that is coming into awareness including thoughts, emotions and sensory perceptions.

Permitting without judgement anything and everything that has a desire of its own to froth up to the surface, but then letting it all go (as best I can), and returning focus back to the deep feeling of my essential being.

Later on, as beingness evolved in me and I regained better control of my impulses, the definition of what meditation was evolved along with it. But first, let's take things one step at a time.

Also, occasionally, I recommend letting the focus dwell on these dissolving words that inhabit the book. Use them as opportunities to take a pitstop, and collect yourself a little deeper in awareness by closing your eyes and taking a few breaths, and watch the focus as it turns inwards, so that now you are reading yourself the same way you were reading the book.

And I will share some simple techniques along the way to help to do this.

The dissolving words are to leave room for you in here, so that it's not entirely about me.

This book starts at the beginning, and then goes backwards from there. Here is that beginning.

Hope you enjoy,

Rob

Portland

ᕙ

It wasn't a course or a work of literature that my friends were into that started me down the road of sitting in stillness; it was loneliness, plain and simple.

When the penny dropped, it was not a sunny day.

I was in Portland. Which is in Oregon, which is in the USA. Staring out the window at the biggest snowstorm in twenty years.

The city had had to borrow snowploughs from Seattle because they weren't equipped for a blizzard this big. In one afternoon, 11.8 inches of snow fell. The governor of Oregon, Kate Brown, called a state of emergency, and the whole state came to a standstill. Not that anyone could've gotten very far – down my quiet street it was up to five feet. Vast slabs of snow sat heaving off the rooftops of all the cars.

Our night's filming had been cancelled, and tomorrow's forecast meant that tomorrow night's would likely fare the same.

My lodging at the time was one of those post-human all-mod-cons short-term-rental revolving doors that photograph well, but where all the warmth and signs of humanity have been stripped away. There was a futon, a 'smart' television, a fitted kitchen complete with glassy dining table set, and an en-suite double bedroom upstairs.

Gazing out the window of what had been the latest 'home' for about a week now, my mind was doing backflips. I was screaming silently at myself: 'I've just watched *Jaws* – now what? I've got two more whole days to kill alone?! What on Earth am I going to do? Watch another movie that I'm supposed to have seen, or maybe put on my coat, hat and boots and go outside and make snow angels? But what then? Survey them proudly by myself? Pretend that I'm standing next to myself and nudge myself on the elbow and say, "Well done"?'

I was in Portland for the specific task of making a movie. Previous to this movie, within the space of a year, I'd hopped non-stop across the world making other movies in New Orleans, Berlin, east Iceland and Western Australia, with stop-offs in London, Los Angeles and San Francisco along the way. After my time in Portland was through, I was scheduled to hop across the world again to Wellington, New Zealand, to make another movie, for what would turn out to be seven months.

Up to that point in Portland I'd been fine, or so I'd thought. There was plenty of work stuff to keep my days busy-buzzy-busy, and then night shoots or dinner/drinks were keeping most evenings occupado. Portland was my latest brand-new place, which meant a brand-new adventure, which meant more than enough justification to fill up my experience cup as close to the brim as humanly possible.

Put another way, I had comfortably managed to avoid confronting my growing loneliness at all costs, until the worst blizzard in twenty years forced me to.

The day was the 10th of January 2017, a white day in Portland history, when I was hit with the chilling realisation that I had become completely incapable of being alone with myself. This chill hit me not so much like an avalanche, but more like a snowflake.

Incapable of being alone ... With myself? Put that way, it sounded odd. Like the sound of the refrigerator light clicking on and echoing across the empty kitchen.

It's like what Bill Burr said: 'I used to think I was really driven, and now I realise I just can't bear to be alone with my thoughts.' Ouch, Bill. You nailed me in one, and made me giggle while doing it, you dream-weaver.

Somewhere along the road when I wasn't looking, my nerves had severely shortened. I'd got to the point where if I was left on my own, even for a short while, I was a twitching mess. Scratching at the walls and dragging my ass along the floor.

And an imperceptible layer of unpleasant static noise had developed over the top of everything. Feral thinking, which mostly didn't benefit me. Thinking was only really of benefit to me if I stopped and thunk the thoughts with some degree of will, but left to their own devices my endless thinkings were only serving to dilute the joy in my life.

'Well, isn't that troubling ...' I thought. 'If my mind is this demanding and chaotic when it's not absorbed in anything, how on Earth am I supposed to get any real peace or enjoyment out of life? Work is going great. I am getting what I am asking for there, and yet by pursuing and achieving this desire that I have so long harboured, an equal and opposite misery is growing, one that I'm having to just get used to and make concessions for and sedate more and more as the days roll by.' It was the old road retrodden: the harder I worked, the more success I experienced, the more impoverished I became.

Behind or above or below the performance of my day – work, play, sleep, travel, exercise, groom, make dinner, argue or make up with significant other, surf social media or play mind-numbing little games on my phone – festered the knowledge that the more I ignored myself by constantly giving myself what I wanted, the less control I would have over my desire to get it.

I was in need of too many things to feel happy. I had become so tired of always looking ahead. So sick of pursuing things all the time, wearied by perpetually trying to 'better my lot', as though it was proper to live in a constant state of needing bettering all the time.

Half the time, during that time, I didn't know whose suitcase I was unpacking. Checking in in the latest hotel lobby, I was (in) a hologram who was flickering on and off six inches above the floor. And now, as I squinted through the fog of jet lag out my latest window, apart from the snow I recognised nothing of the street I was on. And when I went out for a solo stroll to explore my local area, the world felt distant and strange and far away, like virtual reality.

I walked around to actively ignore the feeling that I had falsely inherited this life from someone I'd never met, and that any minute now a website administrator would notice their error, fix the glitch, and switch us back.

I craved being with other people, even though I was becoming more and more averse to the bullshit that would come tumbling out of my own (alleged) mouth. I related less and less to the decisions I was making, but I didn't know how to make any new ones.

I was like an automaton, moving towards things that provided (short-term) pleasure, and running away from things that created stress.

This feeling was gnawing away at my chest. It was taking little bites out of my ankles and nibbling my shins like a cartoon cat eating a spare rib.

It glowered behind the curtain like a ghost, putting a real dampener on the effortless enjoyment of my day, because when a ghost like that is ignored long enough, everything else becomes its opposite. Privately, I wondered whether I still had the capacity to be happy anymore without any assistance, be it visual, chemical or squeezable, and was too scared to put that question to the test.

And without that courage it got to: 'Well, if real, lasting peace is an impossibility then fine, so be it, but I'm sure as hell not going to be miserable either.'

I remember in Iceland standing in front of a spectacular panoramic view of snow-capped glacial mountains with beautiful crystalline-blue lakes at their feet, and flocks of wild Atlantic birds swooped majestically along the vertical precipices, but instead of being filled with simple, effortless wonder, it made me feel uneasy.

And frustrated. Because the beauty was so large in dimension, so awe-inspiring in majesty, I decided that my tiny brain couldn't *possibly* possess the necessary software required to absorb all of it. So I couldn't relax. I had to really make an *effort* to enjoy the beauty, pulling and dragging at it in vain attempts to try to 'get the best out of it', all the while wishing that one day in the vague future, I would possess greater processing power so as to better absorb beauty in full. But, until that time came, I'd just have to continue feeling inferior in the presence of it. How absurd.

Unwittingly, I was using the smallest part of my mind to do something that it's not designed to do, and as such, this cool, glamorous life that I was living, this fantastical journey across the world, was sort of being lost on me. Because even the simplest appreciation of beauty was tangled up with a painful sense of inadequacy.

So, to sedate these gnawing feelings, I used too much alcohol and weed, and other human beings for casual sex.

> 'True prayer and love are learned in that hour when prayer becomes impossible and the heart has turned to stone.'

Thomas Merton, Buddhist teacher

It wasn't that I suddenly dropped to my knees and arrived at prayer and love on the 10th of January 2017. It was more like turning around and noticing that there was a giant African elephant standing next to the futon, and realising he'd been there the whole time.

Staring out at the incessant snowfall, rocking back and forth, I found myself removed from myself.

'Who is this person who is causing me all this suffering anyway? Why can't I stand to be alone with him?'

I thought getting what you wanted was supposed to feel good . . . ?

When I was a child, I possessed 'notions'. Which, where I'm from, means having an overly inflated sense of yourself. Credit in part due to my mother, Maria, who showered me with a mother's love, and voiced many times how wonderful and beautiful I was as a babe.

I remember being six years old. Drifting around a sporting goods store in my local town of Portlaoise, and vowing to myself that for the rest of my days I would only *ever* buy and wear luminous clothing. Not exactly the promise of a shrinking violet. I was enamoured at the time by Mexico's Jorge Campos, who was guarding the goals in the 1994 soccer World Cup in the USA. He was so flamboyant and expressive, decked out from top to bottom in a luminous, baggy, multicoloured goalkeeping kit that would have made an Amazonian bird-of-paradise blush. And always kissing his gloves and gesticulating dramatically up to the sky, like god herself was on his side and had been instrumental in helping him stop the opposition's latest penalty kick.

Later in life, I have a sneaking suspicion that these irrational 'notions' of mine, notions that I was destined for more, strangely helped when it came to pursuing a career in showing off (acting) . . .

I had a bent for the dramatic from the get-go. Even long before tasting the stage drug. Once, as a nipper of about eight or nine, after taking proper umbrage at some parental decision or other, I decided I was better off alone and promptly ran away from home. After climbing out my narrow bedroom window, I sat outside our driveway on a low concrete wall next to the house under an orange streetlamp. In my lap sat a full loaf of sliced white bread stuffed into a drawstring bag. It was all I thought to bring as I set off into the world to make a new life by myself. My mother came down the drive and sat next to me, and gently tried to persuade me to come back in the house, though leaving the decision firmly up to me so as to maintain my dignity. After about an hour, and the cold night chill cutting right through me, the absurdity of my predicament dawned and I relented, and cancelled the running away, because by then I had received sufficient amounts of the thing that I had really been pursuing anyway, which was attention.

I was a curious lad. I craved the company of others when I was alone, yet felt anxiety when in the company of others. I could've been classified as a social contrarian: I needed people around just to disagree with them. That part hasn't changed much.

It was nothing out of the ordinary for me to feel paralysed by a dose of nerves when meeting someone new. Faced with a stranger, particularly one my own age, my body would react as though there was a good chance that it was about to be attacked. My little auto-animal would emerge, baring its teeth and arching its back, and it was my job to conceal it. To draw the curtain quickly across it and give off that I felt just fine. Later on in life, I would use this same bizarre strategy to approach the art of acting.

'Everybody is so cool on television,' I thought. 'They are loved and admired, so maybe if I'm on television this strange feeling that there are no words for and no way to express will go away.'

That's why the camera was there even before it was.

I remember summertime, wandering around in our backyard presenting imaginary television shows. My brother, Brendan, and his friend had put two jumpers down on the grass, and were timing themselves doing sprints. I took my audience up to the starting line – 'On your marks, get set, go!' – and took off running, all the while still presenting my TV show to the imaginary camera crew who were running along beside me trying not to trip over imaginary cables. I was only snapped out of it when Bren looked at me quizzically: 'Who are you talking to?'

I loved other people selfishly, because being around them was the key to being a version of myself that I aspired to be. A version that I could not be on my own. And so, fatalistically, I accepted that these very difficult, primal feelings that came up when around other people was just the tax I had to pay. A tax that everyone paid, presumably . . . ?

What other conclusion could a young fellow draw, looking around at his hyper-social community?

Everyone carrying on together and having the craic, laughing and singing, making it look like it was the easiest thing in the world. At just nine years old, you'd have found me out in a country pub playing Irish traditional music until all hours on a Monday night. The school headmaster/puppeteer, Des, knew this, and would permit me to come in a little later on Tuesday mornings. The pub was called Turley's, long since closed down, and sat along the Barrow line of the Grand Canal of Ireland, which connects Dublin city to the River Shannon. It was all barges and houseboats, and every Monday night the moon would be bouncing off the water and the rafters would be bouncing off of Turley's. All who came were welcome, punters and musicians alike, and every week you had the same locals arriving to sing the same songs: 'Give us a song there, Liam!' 'Go on there, Micheál.' And if ever I was called out to play a solo tune on the tin whistle – 'Robbie, give us a blast of "The Lonesome Boatman"!' – my head would go redder than the packet of cheese-and-onion Taytos splayed open on the pub table. I was so young, I remember falling hook, line and sinker for my brother's 'I can pull off my own thumb' trick. The penny finally dropped when he performed the thumb-removal procedure to others, clearly feeling no pain at all.

In the midst of all that craic, surrounded by members of my own community, I could never fully relax and join in.

Even on a rare day among friends, all of us galloping around in the sun playing soccer together over the road in the local housing estate, seemingly out of nowhere that same familiar ghoul of unpleasant self-awareness was known to shroud itself over me like an invisible veil. And then I'd stop playing soccer and feel sad and withdraw. Because it meant that the day's fun was over, because there was nothing I could do to shake the feeling, because the veil was stubborn, and I never knew when it might lift.

Before sitting in undistracted spaciousness became enjoyable, I had absolutely no understanding of what 'being' meant, on its own or otherwise. I didn't know that being, on its own, existed, let alone that it had value. Round my way growing up, its value was referred to as 'god', which was confusing.

If I had conjured to mind the concept of 'beingness' or 'stillness' and examined its contents (which I wouldn't have done), I'd have been met with maybe at best an image of a still lake glittering in the sunshine. But I certainly would not have included myself in the picture. And also, what would not have accompanied the image was any kind of feeling in the body. Like the warm, tingly feeling earned from experience. Like if you asked a skydiver to conjure to mind a game of polo versus asking them to conjure jumping out of an airplane. For the polo they might render a passable picture of a cluster of horse-mounted players all clattering and clashing mallets and sending divots of earth flying up into the air. But for the skydiving, a whole body's worth of textured memories would emerge as they began to relive the experience of leaping out of a plane.

I once leapt out of a plane in eastern Australia. I'd just been paid, and had just broken up with the first love of my life for good after many practice break-ups. And there was an exhilaration of freedom lacquered over the top of a repressed misery, so on a whim I decided to jet off to the other side of the world to go and celebrate my pal's twenty-first birthday, by bouncing around hostels and getting drunk for six weeks.

And when I say 'leapt out of a plane', I was limply strapped to another, larger man like a vestigial limb.

On that morning, I was shaken from sleep, having been up the whole night before, drinking and dancing around a giant bonfire on a beach. And for some reason I convinced this French fellow called Alex, who was staying in the same dormitory, and who didn't have a word of English, to accompany me. When we got to the little airfield, poor Alex wasn't allowed on the plane, so he just had to stand on the runway alone in the wind and wait for us to float back down to Earth.

Cruising at 14,000 feet, they undid a padlock on a rolling shutter and it clanged open, and suddenly there was a giant gaping hole in the side of the plane. And Nathan, the larger man, was shouting at the top of his lungs over the engines: 'Now! Lip your legs right around the side of the plane, and we'll go on three, alright? Ready? One . . . Fuck it – GO!'

But the only problem was that in the time it took us to ascend to that height, the clouds had fully rolled in, so on the way down on our fall we saw fuck-all. We were two ragdolls hurtling through a blinding mist. Until we fell below the cloudline, and Nathan pulled the cord, and we were hit with a view so high that we could see the curvature of the Earth. As tears streamed down my cheeks, the waves fizzed and sparkled white off the jagged coastline for miles, and narrow shafts of golden sun broke through the cracks in the cloud blanket above.

After the initial bouts of adrenalised whooping, we continued to float for another twenty minutes or so like dandelion seeds. Long enough that the extreme proximity between Nathan and me got a bit awkward and I felt compelled to make small talk like we were in the elevator of our shared apartment building.

'So, Nathan . . . D'you have far to travel home, or . . . ? Could we see your house from here? Many jumps to do today?' He told me that I was his 2,350th dive.

> 'Then came the day that he understood
> what language was – a bridge between the
> flesh and the spirit.'
>
> Dermot Healy, *A Goat's Song*

Anyway, all these words on the subject of words versus experience are to bang a bit more on the same drum before we move on.

Dear friend,

If you don't already, why not also try practising a little stillness along with me?

Don't believe a word of mine. If this book is sitting in your lap, then I dare say it means that there is already the seed of curiosity in you.

Water that seed as you read, and then watch it begin to grow little tendrils. No need to put any kind of schedule on it. In my view, there is never a bad moment in the day.

The power of your sight, when you close your eyes and turn it inwards, is potent. Watch that power magnify, enough to begin slowing the oscillation of the particles of your body and mind down to a lower, more spacious vibration. And no matter what guidance you receive along your journey, helpful or no, you are ultimately always your own navigator.

Like St Brendan the Navigator was, when he realised that it wasn't an island he'd camped everyone on, it was the back of a sleeping whale. You sitting duck, St Brendan!

Were not the signs of a huge sea creature apparent as you were setting up your tents? Glistening silvery and smooth under the light of the moon? Sure, you must have been a bit tired from a hard day's rowing across the sea, but what about the fact that there were no shrubs or rocks around? Were not the lungs of the land heaving up and down under your feet?

It must've been very disorienting for poor St Brendan and his crew of monks, when their campfire was dowsed by a big spray of water coming barrelling out of the ground like a fireman's hose, shooting up like a geyser out of a small slurping hole. Was that when the penny dropped?

I wonder how the round-up meeting went in the boat after.

St Brendan: 'Brothers … Now, I know ye're upset that your suppers got washed away. God has never led us this far astray. Yes, he has put us through some challenging trials, but it's safe to say this is probably the ultimate one – camping us down for the night on the back of a giant whale. Now come on, hands together, let us all pray. Hands, Diarmuid! May the Devil bleach that fearsome Jaconius, and beach the foul creature, that all his descendants be prevented from ever getting to swim in the sea. Amen.'

And along the way, I share some simple, useful techniques that helped me along the voyage, but in the end, you make all your own mistakes and all your own breakthroughs. You are your most important teacher. You are St Brendan, you are the whale, you're the first mate, the cook, the masseuse, the shantyman, and the parrot sitting on your own shoulder.

This is not a voyage that relies on technology, or the night sky, or a book, or any other external thing. Down in the depths of profound purposelessness the universe offers plenty of guidance from within. It is a trip that can only set sail once all the rest has been put aside.

So go on, give the practice a promotion from polo to skydiving.

ß

There once was a monk called Bell,

Who floated in light-form gel,

By the hem of his robes

He furrowed his nose,

And whiffed a vermilion-y smell.

Now I am grateful to that twenty year blizzard. For putting down such a blanket of quiet to start me off. She was my ally. Have you noticed that when it snows, it quietens down the world?

In my all-mod-cons rental in Portland, as darkness was falling and the storm was finally subsiding, I decided that all of this disconnect I was feeling was because of the cartoonish amounts of international travel, and the constant work, and the long stretches of time away from what was familiar to me. So, I thought, what better way to have a direct experience of/with reality than to sit by myself in a darkened room, with no distractions, and face head-on into the wind of it and see what happens. To see if I could face into it long enough for the storm to eventually pass. So I went upstairs to the en-suite double bedroom, lit a candle, put the lights down low, and sat cross-legged on my bed.

I had some intuition that the act of just sitting there in that sterile bedroom, closing my eyes and trying to look at myself would be akin to walking a tightrope. One that I was definitely going to fall off at least the first hundred times I tried. And for that reason, it was permissable to completely delay all judgement, either good or bad, of the progress I was making.

As I got settled and the candle flame flickered against the teal-painted wall, I felt an unexpected wave of nauseous fear wash through me, and realised that I felt scared to be looking at myself. I was worried that I would not like what I found. That my mental chatter would be too raw, too pathetic, too painful, and that I would tell myself things about myself, things that I wouldn't be able to unthink.

And after the first few moments of collecting myself passed, when my mind realised that it was being deprived of being absorbed by something other than itself, it mutinied. It harumphed and moaned that I *needed* to pick up my phone and text that person. It *screamed* and *pulled* and *dragged* at my body, complaining that there was that script I ought to be reading, and scolded: 'What is the point of just sitting here doing all this nothing when there are so many things to do?'

And when a thought crossed my mind, I thought that that meant I had made a mistake and had failed, and that now I had to clear my head out and start again from scratch once back in 'pure black'. But this time, really *clench* my mind shut until it got the message to stop! I thought the purpose of practising meditation was to push and pull my mind around like I would with weights down the gym. To get my mind in a chokehold, essentially, until it blacked out.

It was the same with stretching. I used to be a terror for over-stretching. Restless Rob had a tendency to always want to *get* somewhere with it. To get deeper into that stretch, and as soon as possible! Always trying to expedite my flexibility progress, and as a result I'd ended up slowing down my progress considerably.

I was yet to understand that if a body stretch was making my face do a stretch, it meant I was doing it too hard, and things had gone from stretching to suffering-management.

Perversely, I suspect part of me enjoyed the outset of meditation precisely because it hurt so much to do so. In terms of 'personal improvement', my belief at the time was that if it wasn't hurting, it meant it wasn't working.

So I laboured away under the illusion that the job required was to march 'in there', grab all the painful thorns (the unwanted thoughts and unpleasant feelings), and *yank* them out like some kind of medieval torture.

But it turns out that that whole approach was tantamount to pissing into a barrel of sawdust, as they say around my way. And instead, the trick was to flip it, and begin *accepting* all of the perceived thorns fully, which in turn gave the skin a chance to soften so that they would fall out of their own accord.

After just a few minutes I could no longer take the intense cold of silence. So I stuck on a guided YouTube meditation video of some young American guy with a hilariously ominous voice. Every line was delivered as though we were sitting at dinner and through gritted teeth he was trying to tell me that there was a bomb under the table. 'Concentrate on that which is unchanging withinnn.'

The longer I sat twitching in that austere bedroom trying to think 'nothing', the more the thoughts bulged and popped like balloons inside my skull. It was like the Game, which my pal Ronnie taught me: 'Alright, you are now officially playing the Game. And you can never, *ever* win the Game. But every time you remember that you're playing the Game, you have lost the Game.'

It was like that, except that the Game was every single mental form that galloped into my mind, and all of the aftershocks of post-analyses of each of those mental forms. Ego future fantasies (scenarios in which I cast myself as heroic and cool in some potential future) walloped me between the eyes like they'd been fired out of a catapult from somewhere in the darkness ahead. Ego past fantasies (scenarios in which I relived events that had already happened, but this time said or did something to make the other people in the memory think that I was powerful and that they were smaller than me) dragged me kicking and screaming out of the room before dumping me back onto the bed when they were finished with me.

And after it all went out again, like the tide, even the blankness of my remaining thoughtlessness, the 'black screen', now felt uncomfortable. Because even when the mad newsreel of thoughts had receded for a few moments, and I was delivered back to my present bedroom, its absence somehow felt just as conspicuous as its presence. Its absence created an unpleasant anticipatory static electric charge in my head.

Like restless leg syndrome, if you've ever had that. It feels like sudden surges of uncomfortable sensation racking the branches of nerves in your legs, demanding movement. This is what meditation felt like in the beginning: restless mind syndrome.

And each thought arrived with a million satellites around it, most of which I could sense but all of which were invisible because I'd never taken the time to travel to them.

It was like my imagination was solely in the jurisdiction of my ego. So those first waves of imagination coming in were not fun at all. They were erratic, petty, punitive, worrisome and needlessly competitive, and I did not feel as though they accurately reflected my true nature. I was afraid of what my imagination might show me next.

It seems that my ego, in terms of how it wields my imagination, is mostly interested in securing a version of the future that makes me seem superior to other people. Or rewriting the past, but again, in more triumphant themes.

No matter how hard I tried, I could not stop my mind making demands, presenting unwanted memories, and versions of myself specifically to do with other people. And asking endless puzzling questions like, 'How does my mind work anyway? How can it ask itself all these questions? That must mean that there is an asker and a receiver . . . But then, am I fundamentally the one who is asking the question or the one who is receiving the question? Or is it that the receiver is asking himself the question? But if that's the case, why would I ask myself a question that I know I don't know the answer to? And why, in quiet moments, does my mind feel the need to remind me of many of the things that caused me some pain or other? Why would I not remind myself of the joys just as quickly? And why is my mind on autopilot anyway? It's annoying and distracting. Can there realistically be a way of being completely without it? And if so, would there *really* be any great benefit to switching it off?'

What good's the name afforded you,

When all the world has flown from view?

What form must body dwindle to,

But colour of black with streaks of blue?

Wherefore should now my flesh cling to?

And what, pray tell, is it fastened to?

My breath has billowed out my name,

Flesh gone to vap'rous billows same.

While gone I see they're both see-through,

And oh!

What streaks of black and purplish blue ...

Around and around and around, and on and on my mind went, like a carousel. Thoughts rippling outwards endlessly and crashing into one another, like the surface of a pond after hurling in a fistful of pebbles.

Outwards from an imagined future to a thought about the fact that my mind had just dragged me to an imagined future. And then to an image of me telling people in an imagined future about how my mind is always dragging me to imagined futures.

And sometimes the thoughts were explosive, and acted as the catalyst to transmit very unpleasant emotions into my body. Thoughts that were destructive in nature, and made it clear to me the pattern they wanted my life to go, and it was one that included conflict. 'But why do I imagine these things that I know in my heart of hearts I do not want?' Were these thoughts really mine?

And when these fantasies dragged me out of the present, either to the future or the past, and completely consumed my attention, I felt a wave of shrinking, strickening duality come over me. Like I'd been torn in half.

Despite my designs to voluntarily fall off the tightrope and defer all judgement of my progress, I couldn't help despairing in self-pity. That I had discovered the thing I most feared to be true: that I am one of the wretched souls who has drawn the short straw by having a ceaselessly restless mind. A mind that does not switch off.

Implicit in the statement 'I cannot switch my mind off' is instant failure. A belief that if my mind does what it does naturally, and secretes a thought or an emotion or two while trying to remain in delicious spaciousness, this makes a failure of the whole enterprise. But there is no such thing as failure or success per se, it is an ongoing practice, like eating food or doing yoga, meaning the journey continues until death do ye part. There is no A trying to get to some B, because there is just A.

I once was told that muscular pain the day after training is just 'weakness leaving the body'. Little did I know at the outset of my meditation practice that all of this incoherent mental activity was just weakness leaving the mind.

There was a study that came out of Goldsmiths, University of London, called 'Relaxing Learned Constraints through Cathodal tDCS on the Left Dorsolateral Prefrontal Cortex', and I thought, 'Dang, that's what I wanted to call this book.' Transcranial direct current stimulation (tDCS) is a procedure that stimulates and activates brain cells by delivering electrical signals. It's used as a treatment for a variety of different ailments including anxiety, PTSD and depression.

In the case of the Goldsmiths study, they were trying to see if they could improve the rates of problem-solving in test subjects by alleviating the left prefrontal cortex, the part of the brain that is to do with problem-solving. To see if new solutions to things would arise just by relaxing the constraints of formerly learned rules.

The results showed compelling evidence that we are so much more creative when our minds are clearer, less referential of the past, more spontaneous and more at peace. As though we draw the newness of inspiration out of the ether.

'Ether' is a beautiful word. It stems from the word 'aether' which, in the fourth century BC, Aristotle believed was a fifth element that made up the substance of the celestial bodies that surrounded our own in outer space.

By the early seventeenth century, René Descartes was using the word 'aether' to symbolise the medium of space itself.

Our brains demand more energy than any other organ in the body. They are enormous processers, still unknowably complex. And a brain that is constantly thinking is, as Dr David Spiegel, the director of the Center on Stress and Health at Stanford put it, '. . . like running your car in the wrong gear. Your motor's running but you're not getting very far.'

Engaging in overthinking all day long, like I was (and am still known to do now and then, occasionally), puts us under excessive stress. It depletes the brain's and body's natural functions. The complementary fight/flight response that goes along with thinking too much suppresses our inspired creative problem-solving side. It affects our quality of sleep, stifles the imagination, and prevents us from committing events clearly to memory. Stay up in one's head long enough, and eventually one becomes a stranger to oneself.

'Mr Duffy ... lived at a little
distance from his body.'

James Joyce, 'A Painful Case'

Health of body and health of mind are one and the same, to the extent that it's all but negligible to split them into two. They have been separated for the purposes of study, but for all intents and purposes they are not. That is why, in my view, we would be better off reunionising the words, when referring to oneself, back to 'bodymind'.

'Je pense, donc je suis
[I think, therefore I am].'

René Descartes

Arguably the statement that formed the basis of all Western philosophy from the seventeenth century on.

René reasoned that the only true confirmation of existence, from the standpoint of universal doubt, was thinking. He hitched all of existence to the wagon of thoughts – the holographic representations of reality inside his head.

This is completely back-to-front. It is self-evident that existence carries on unencumbered even when thoughts are not passing through our minds.

But perhaps I'm short-changing René. Perhaps instead of passive thinking (the thoughts that appear on their own and tend to have the engine running in the wrong gear), *'je pense'* for him meant applying his focus to solving a problem. Critical thinking is a different kettle of fish to passive thinking, but it still runs us into the same problem that René was trying to solve by attempting to turn thinking into a kind of guarantee of existence, which is like citing the clouds as proof of the sky.

Also, my opinion of René's attitudes towards existence cannot help but be swayed a touch by the fact that he once nailed his wife's dog by the legs to a wooden board, and then proceeded to cut it open while it was still alive. He was in pursuit of some physical evidence to support his theory that animals do not possess souls in the way that we do. And that any supposed expression of emotion, like pain, is merely pretence. The dog is pretending to be in pain, it cannot actually feel pain, and if it seems like it is, it is only copying humans. In order to trick us so that it can stay alive, as opposed to actually enduring agonising pain for real like we would if we were nailed to a board. It was the early 1600s, and he had a mother who had died a year after he was born, and a daughter who had died five years after she was born. But his reasoning could lead him to places that were undeniably quite fucked up.

In peaceful moments we are simply there, peacefully *not* thinking, contentedly rocking back and forth on the porch watching the sunset with a shotgun in our lap, listening to the needling of crickets and the whoosh of a faraway highway. We are in a state of non-duality. There is no need to convert this pleasant moment in which we are fully aware into abstract symbolic thought in order for it to exist.

'I am, therefore I think.'

Deepak Chopra

Which, for me, intuitively feels like the more accurate sequence.

On our podcast, *The Earth Locker*, discussing his ninety-first book, *Metahuman*, I asked Deepak, 'How do you write books, mate?'

'At night, I just ask myself a few questions before I go to sleep and in the morning I download the answers.'

This approach sits on a bedrock of trust that the human mind goes far beyond just thinking, and that it can retrieve vast amounts of information as long as one operates its interface correctly.

As Deepak declared on *The Earth Locker*, 'What is at the core of a human being? Infinite possibilities, and education is *bringing that out*. Not information overload. If I want information overload, I go to Google.'

Back in snowy Portland, sat in my first ever meditation session, I was drowning in information overload, and in despair over just how stormy my undistracted mind had become. And despite my desire to soothe it by giving it something to eat other than itself, instead I endeavoured to just keep going.

'I can't switch my mind off' is definitely the most common reason people cite when the subject of meditation comes up naturally or is crowbarred into conversations (by me). And it struck me to keep one ear open for other reasons people cite that keep them from practising.

Another common one I've heard is that practising complete purposelessness is associated with laziness. Around my way growing up, it was the culture that if you were found sitting completely still and weren't asleep or dead, it meant there was something wrong with you. Boredom was a sin, and to avoid committing it meant filling the day with useful and productive activites. Sitting very still in a prolonged fashion did not qualify as one of these.

A while back, I was sat in the passenger seat of my pal Dan's car. And as we drove along, he was thinking out loud when he told me he was wary of meditation, 'because it would mean I'd get nothing done'. There was this belief in Dan that just sitting awhile and contemplating inwardly might be enough to bring him to a point where he lost all motivation to continue living his life.

That a little calm and loving surrender to stillness would have such a dire effect that it would sap his ability to get up in the morning and care. In other words, interestingly, Dan feared that practising would make him depressed. Embracing beingness, for Dan, symbolised a step away from life, not towards it.

My other friend Pamela remarked similar, that she didn't fancy meditation because she wanted to 'stay fully in the game'.

I find this is similar to how people say that they don't want to lift too many weights down the gym for fear of getting 'too big'.

Dreading too much result too quickly is an austere way of approaching anything. Nowhere in Dan's ominous fantasy, where he'd suddenly upped sticks, abandoned his wife and children and sold all his possessions and clothes to wander the Earth as a Samana, was there room for everything he already had.

He made me understand how practising being centred and still represents a kind of danger for some. That closely inspecting the grouting will make the tiles start falling off.

Another cause I have encountered holding folks back is that life is busy enough! How can one find the time to devote themselves to meditation amid the temptation artillery of phones, drones, ice-cream cones, girlfriends, boyfriends, social causes, contractual clauses, Etta James, video games, Insta influencer killing the video killing the radio star. Shopping, online shopping, TV shopping, studying degrees and masters, Super Glue and Band-Aid plasters, employees, summer vacations, faulty wirings, sackings and hirings? Rhyme, innit.

A pithy little list there to convey a snowflake's worth of the avalanche of stimulating concepts that the modern world throws at us every day. Life is busy enough. Who has the time to add some blank spaciousness into the daily routine? Most of us get up every day and live life like we've been fired out of a cannon.

From this perspective, 'adding' meditation to the pile seems ludicrous, and for the time required can the benefits really be worth it? To remain still is a luxury of sorts. An activity that might add a little icing on the cake of life, sure – for those who have the privilege of plenty of spare time and no kids (me).

To that I would enquire, how much of life is spent distracting yourself from the present moment by doing things or thinking about the things that you're going to do (while staring at a screen)? When I hear an older person say, 'God, I don't know where the time's gone! It feels like I was twenty-five twenty-five minutes ago,' part of me wonders if it's because they spent their whole life distracted from the present moment by doing things or planning to do the next thing.

Some people, when I have crowbarred the practice of being on its own into our chat, kind of glaze over and mutter under their breath, 'Yeah, I need to meditate more.' Like it's three-quarters of the way down a burdensome mental to-do list. It's akin to going to the doctor's to get that itchy mole you were worried about checked, or re-doing the warped floors in the kitchen. A duty that is worthwhile carrying out, sure, and would make life better, but the thought of actually doing the work inspires something a little more than discomfort and a little less than dread.

Another concern I've noticed is that practising meditation turns you into a prat. Plain and simple. Devoting time to marinating yourself in the simple aliveness of being can consume your personality and reduce your identity to cliché. This is a real pitfall that some temporarily trip into, particularly early on in the practice. I have been this person. And I have met a few of these people at that stage along their road, who seem to have lost a great deal of natural joy, not acquired more of it.

Cautiousness, for all manner of reasons, towards cultivating emptiness is common. It is the product of a talking mind that is reacting to the threat of change. But what is possible to see (but which the talking mind cannot) is that for such dangers to be avoided, they must first be invented.

To my typical waking mind, practising no-mind was to go somewhere that it couldn't follow. Somewhere it wasn't needed. My mind felt its own future jeopardised, and so it painted ominous pictures of what embracing mindfulness might result in.

My mind created stories, albeit compelling ones, to maintain familiar boundaries. Whispering in my ear, 'Tread with caution. If you give less of your focus to me and more of it to what could be there in my absence, I'm not sure if I can still look out for us both. Why change things now? We're still alive, aren't we? Isn't that good enough?'

In the beginning, confronting myself head on did feel risky. In my more cynical mind-led moments, it felt like I was inviting mental and emotional instability upon myself. Like I stood to lose something vital to my sense of self-worth, as opposed to gaining something. I felt like Samson snipping small curls off with a pair of shears.

I was yet to comprehend that to pre-judge the practice of broadening beingness as dangerous, as justification for dismissing it out of hand and never getting beyond the fear of it to give it a real chance, was to embody the belief that 'It is not in my interest to get closer to that which sustains my whole life.' Not the best message to be sending oneself.

In the beginning, delaying judgement one way or the other was crucial in learning how to forgive myself for having such an erratic, incoherent mind. Now, I am grateful to all that static noise too. Because it was the catalyst that led to the pastime of tasting my consciousness evolving into a practice of continual self-forgiveness. A great habit to get into.

Resistance

Swims me to the fringes,

Where the current is less strong,

Where the light is less bright and the shadows

are more long.

In the shallows here it's familiar,

But not necessarily safer in the long run.

In Ireland where I grew up, there's always been a fine line between volume and charm. And as a squirt, I definitely had the two confused. I idolised confident social (loud) behaviour in other boys. The rewarded behaviour was peacockish behaviour. The trick to it seemed to be: who can be the loudest and yet the most natural-seeming at the same time? Who can best mask the inherent discomfort of being around other people?

Who can look like they're having the best time? It didn't matter to me whether or not the peacock was *actually* having a good time. What mattered was how convincing the veneer of their good time was. I envied those who were able to make it seem like they were having a great time, because they inspired me to wonder whether or not they were actually experiencing the same social calcification I was. I'd watch the peacock, and then project my own fantasy onto him: to be among others and not feel cowed by social inhibition. But in the back/front of my mind, I was certain that the peacock was pretending too – he was just better at it than I was – and that gave my little ego a real appetite to improve.

There was one boy, let's call him Will, who was incredibly performative around other people. He had this hyena-pitched giggle, which had the potential to erupt into a shrill, full-throated cackle.

His gregarious energy created around him a kind of orbit. I have a conscious memory now of something that was unconscious at the time, of sitting in a group by the pond in Portlaoise town park, trying to play it cool *and* analyse Will's social cues at the same time, so that later I could use them as my own. His energy output, his instinct towards mockery, his domineering squeaking laugh.

I learned that socialising had to mean performing. It was the only way it could be done with any degree of comfort.

His moves meant everyone else was on the back foot. He made us all feel a little smaller, so to feel bigger I should be more like him.

All of this was happening internally, meaning it was happening emotionally, but not consciously. I was not aware until later how strongly these conclusions were taking root.

Nor was I aware that this archetype of Will would play out in me in some form for a good decade and a half to follow. I would employ his social tactics to evade my own inner discomfort, and eventually I'd get pretty damn good at it.

This approach to life bred a streak of controllingness in me. Always seeking a fair degree of control over a social situation, through whatever means necessary shy of jousting. I had to both feel good and look good in the eyes of *everyone else* in order to be having a truly good time.

When meeting a new person, I always worked harder with them than with people I already knew. I wanted the new person to be wowed. Impressed! By me. I was leaving a residue of myself in their heads so it had to be a trace I could live with, substantial enough not to haunt me in my quieter moments. A person not liking me was a thing I worked far too hard to avoid.

'Roll up, roll up! Look at my wares. Let's play and see how humbled I can make you feel.'

People who are scared of public speaking often become speech-makers. Francis Bacon doubted his ability as a painter. Folks like me, who didn't feel enough socially often become charming as a result. Doubting something results in the need to continually test it. It is a useful raw material. I don't think we give doubt half enough credit.

In later years, that very same Will ended up living on my floor for a time, and he confessed to me how he suffered from bouts of crippling social anxiety.

If I got close to someone romantically, so that they became privy to my most private and most vulnerable life, it seemed, through their eyes, that this charm of mine, which I had put so much effort into, just fell away. It didn't fall away, it flaked off like the surface of a stale old pastry. And then I would feel trapped in the limiting boundary of myself in that person's eyes, and be compelled to run away from her (myself) and re-build my charm anew in someone else's.

And this is why, as a kid, when the couple lived happily after at the end of the rom-com I didn't feel joy, I felt alienated.

After we finally wrapped *Bad Samaritan*, the film we'd been making in Portland, I set sail directly for New Zealand to once again be lead peacock in another movie called *Mortal Engines*. Over the duration of these sevenish months, my practice slowed, because I was working every hour god sent. Up at 6am every day, in time to see the sun rising over the booming waves which rolled and crashed onto the shore directly across the road from my little house. New Zealand is a profoundly elemental place. Everywhere you look there are beautiful, vibrant expressions of nature jostling into one another, not dissimilar to the west coast of Ireland. And if there was a free day at the end of my week, I would use it to party or go off exploring up and down the country to party elsewhere. So, my practice slowed, and didn't resume fully until I found myself in Toronto on the next job – a TV series called *The Umbrella Academy*.

Aside from beginning to feel great beyond words, the practice was now also proving to be an incredibly useful tool in researching my character, Klaus. So during those six months we filmed season one, I returned to the practice with mucho gusto.

'Twas during this time I discovered how, interestingly, my first religious experiences in life were performative, and my first performative experiences were religious.

Mum took us to church until I was tenish. Frantic Sunday mornings spent running around the house looking for the other black shoe. My father Joe, like his father Joe, never went.

Later on, she confessed to me that her main motivation in taking us wasn't to turn us into little soldiers of Christ; it was to uphold a certain community expectation.

Where she was reared, if her Clan weren't in their usual attendance every Sunday morning, the parish would be alive with gossip.

Catholic Mass for me (extremely camp costumes and decor aside) was a monotonous affair. Not so much the practice of social connection but more social compliance, and the sermons inspired not so much spiritual fervour but more a lapse into catatonia.

Week in, week out it was the same thing; the church full of paritioners, zombying through the motions, mumbling the prescribed responses to the prompts of a preoccupied priest. Then we'd all line up in the aisles, heads obediently bowed, to kneel at the altar and receive on the tongue the little white slip of a cracker that was drier than the back of a camel's ballbag. I was always vaguely jealous that the priest got to take a big swig of wine out of that great fancy goblet. I thought the rest of us could've done with a swig to help us wash that cracker down. I remember a neighbour of ours telling me really seriously how her uncle was suing the church, because the priest had stuck the cracker so far down his throat he'd nearly choked to death. I wonder if that case ever made it to court . . .

I decided early on that rational comprehension of Catholicism was not what was being asked of me, and without rational comprehension it offered nothing. Other people carried on like they had some kind of grasp of it all, but I just accepted my duty to be bored. Because, after all, it was only a half-hour a week, and it did allow me to stare at large groups of people sitting (relatively) still.

Only the singing had the power to conjure some real god in me. I loved singing in the choir, and even more so when my voice folded into multipart harmonies with other voices. Singing in harmony with the choir thrilled my whole body and made it fizz like pop rocks. And when I wasn't singing, I would sit in the pews and tune out of the ceremonial drone to people-watch. This is a pastime which remains as absorbing to me as ever, one which is an endless source of inspiration for my job. Watching people sat there in the pews, eyes forward, shifting their weight around to cope with a sore arse, or shifting their eyes to focus inwards to escape the gnawing boredom. Or the silent, desperate mutterings of hurried prayers under the breath with eyes pinched shut, fingering rosary beads, as if the more prayers they managed to get through before the end of Mass, the more likely god was to answer.

At ten years old, my first (and only) paid improv gig took place in the Confession box.

By order of our teacher, Sister Áine, who would go cross-eyed whenever she shouted at us, so much so that we'd be daring each other to wind her up in attempts to make it happen, we were to take our first Confession. It was really to tee us up and get us prepped for the pomp and ceremony of our upcoming Holy Communion, which, after baptism, is the second of the sacraments to reinforce your initiation into the Catholic club.

For those of you raised around other doctrines, Confession is a Catholic ritual where you sit in one side of a small wooden cubicle and a priest sits in the other. You are divided by a slatted partition in the middle, which acts as a visual metaphor for the notions of anonymity and confidentiality.

In Confession, the idea is to alleviate one's conscience by speaking out loud that which is pressing on it. On paper it makes total sense. To disempower the issues of the conscience, issues we all face at different times, is an act of catharsis, meaning to experience relief by letting something go. It is a necessary therapy, and is as universal to being human as growing toenails.

For our first Confession we were to write down on a secret list the sins we had committed, and then recite them to the priest, and the whole thing was framed as a kind of field trip. Albeit a mysterious one, insofar as I hadn't the foggiest, nor cared much, about what it was all supposed to mean. Sister Áine would say things like, 'The sacrament of Confession is an act of worship, to affirm one's willingness to commune with God.'

Commune with money, more like. The chief motivating factor for kids receiving the holy sacraments in Ireland in the 1990s was financial. Other than my first promise of real cash, the whole thing felt abstract and separate from real life. And besides, I was ten and had no real sins to tell. I wished I had something more worthy of the priest's time, like one of the suggestions held up in the Ten Commandments.

I hadn't once coveted any of our neighbours' livestock, or committed adultery or murder. But I had definitely desecrated the odd Sabbath and had learned how to take the big fellow's name in vain with great skill. But I also wasn't too inclined to go into the whole truth and nothing but with the priest, because my conscience was clear enough that I did not yet understand the nature of catharsis, and therefore didn't understand the benefits of confessing. And also, I didn't yet possess the equipment to reflect inwardly in that way. I had only a few words to name the different states of my inner landscape. The language used in the Catholic doctrine might as well have been in Finnish. Most of the words I had to describe my emotions were got from watching television.

So, I got to the front of the queue and shuffled into the little box, and confessed to how I had lied to my sister, Shauna, which was true. And how I had stolen money out of her piggy bank, which wasn't yet true.

The priest, god keep him, who'd spent the whole afternoon fielding herds of unruly children muttered, 'Say ten Hail Marys and ten Our Fathers.' And boom. For our brief improvisational performance piece, I amassed a grand total of fifty-six Irish punts. For the ensuing Holy Communion ceremony, my mother dressed me up in a pimpin' little tweed suit.

Left to right: Brendan, Joe, Me, Maria and Shauna

And the purity of that money was burning such a hole in the pocket of those sweet checkered slacks that I marched straight downtown as soon as the ceremony was done and bought a tennis racket, for some reason.

The only other time I've set foot in Confession since was in Bulgaria, when I was forcibly removed from an old Russian Orthodox church called St Nicholas the Miracle-Maker. The big potato-headed security guard, who smelt oddly of copper coins, found me sitting inside an empty Confession booth wearing a skimpy sleeveless vest, baggy patterned yoga pants and flip-flops. He shooed me out of the box, grunting and thumbing at the church's dress code sign. And when I appealed to his Christian side by requesting he give me a few more minutes, without warning, he shoved and rough-handled me right down the steep steps and out the arched entrance doorway. Once I'd staggered outside and retrieved one of my flip-flops, he made the sign of a cross in the air with his big pink hand. Presumably as a sarcastic blessing?

As I walked away my ego boiled with vivid, illicit fantasies of going back there and teaching him and the whole church a lesson.

It is pertinent to note that by the time I was tenish, the Catholic Church was falling into disrepute. In Ireland, trust in the Church as a guiding light through times of change was being revoked due to our culture being flooded with all the reports of child abuse. I remember Ireland's *Late Late Show* being on the TV at home, the longest-running live chat show in the world, and being hit with a jarring disruption as grown adults, men in their forties, were standing up in the audience in floods of tears to share their accounts of abuse carried out by members of the clergy.

And further reports followed of the higher-ups of the Roman Catholic empire being complicit in the cover-ups of these incidents.

So by the time we were channelled through the dog-and-pony show, its influence was in major decline.

In the breath of one generation, the Church went from being the cornerstone of society to a dusty old arch-roofed building full of perverts. And I cite the Church not to be accusatory, but because they were and still are the only real spiritual game in my town. Our town's only public space meant for us all to connect in a way that doesn't require words.

Putting its past aside, nowadays at thirty-six-ish, the Church makes a lot more sense.

It's the only building typically where members of a community get to bow their heads together in (relative) quiet.

It can be quite a moving experience now, going to Mass at home. At Christmas, their busiest night of the year, the place is packed to the rafters with young and old, many standing at the back for want of seats. Still quite boring, though.

I'm curious to know if Portlaoise or any other church would go the whole hog and entertain the notion of having a 'quiet Mass'? A no-speaking sermon, one that permits and encourages the silence between us, like the way composer John Cage's silent piece, '4' 33"', is embraced in a concert hall. To speak no word is to betray no doctrine.

And perhaps there could also be some complementary instrumental sound. So instead of praying to god, asking god for stuff, we become god. We become in tune, like the way we used to singing the harmonies in the choir.

And now, a reading from the Gospel of Thomas. Interestingly, the Gospel of Thomas was only discovered in 1945, in Egypt. It's referred to as the 'Coptic gospel', and is a 'sayings gospel', meaning solely a collection of brill things Jesus said. It is a list of 114 of Jesus's best bumper stickers.

Here is one such one: when asked, 'When will the kingdom come, Jesus? This kingdom of heaven you speak of?' Jesus said, 'The kingdom of heaven is spread upon the Earth, but men do not see it.'

Jesus taught folks to be love, as opposed to continually looking for it.

He wasn't half cryptic at times too, though. Or at least, the Coptic sayings that are accredited to him are. I love that heaven quote above because I can relate to it, but it's a little harder to relate to: 'Blessed is the lion that's eaten by a human and then becomes human, but how awful for the human who's eaten by a lion, and the lion becomes human.'

I love the idea of Jesus lounging under a tree mumbling about being eaten by a lion with vague dread, and then one of the sleeping apostles gets a kick: 'Quick, he's saying something. Something about lions!' And with a groggy head, the sleepy apostle grabs papyrus and a reed, and takes it down a bit wrong.

One thing I wonder is: did Jesus practise meditation? How to turn on the tap of eternal love, you ask? The sensation of deepening spaciousness feels like tuning in to the heavenly father or, what the physicist and creator of Transcendental Meditation Maharishi Mahesh Yogi called 'the natural cosmic intelligence'.

Back in the early 1980s, after Bhagwan Rajneesh gave up all hopes of ever being the leader of an Oregon-based world religion, he moved back to India, set up an organisation far quieter and more low key, and began again as Osho.

Of prayer, Osho said this:

I am against prayer. I am for meditation. And
these are the only two dimensions: prayer,
the false dimension; meditation, the right
dimension. In prayer you try first to imagine a
god there, and then you project a prayer. In
meditation you don't have to project any god,
you don't have to believe in any god, you
don't have to utter a single word of prayer. On
the contrary, you move inwards. In prayer
you are moving outwards: a god there ... and
then a bridge of prayer between you and god.
In meditation you have no god there. You
search within ... Taste your consciousness in
silence and peace.

The practice of tasting your consciousness directly is, in many
respects, prayer's opposite.

Prayer	A thing you say. In the form of requests to seduce the will of someone to improve your lot or the lot of the ones you love.
Meditation	Not requesting nothing. Your focus is solely on what energy is there inside yourself and is available all by itself.

Prayer	The practice of asking for help with your life.
Meditation	The practice of calmly witnessing your life.

Prayer	A thing that once it's been 'answered' can result in feelings of spiritual debt which must be repaid.
Meditation	Asks no questions and requires no answers.

Prayer	Makes you separate from god, and puts you automatically beneath god in power and importance/powerlessness and unimportance.
Meditation	No altar required. You are the altar. And the hierarchical scoreboard is seen for what it is. You and god and whatever other concept you dream up all share one importance.

Prayer	A form of simple, quiet talking to our beloved dead.
Meditation	Can be the same.

Prayer	A means of reminding ourselves that there are forces beyond our control which have a profound impact on our lives. Arguably, a larger impact than the one we are making ourselves.
Meditation	The same.

Prayer	Feels good to speak to someone of great silence who never needs to offer a reply.
Meditation	Same.

Despite slagging off prayer, I still say them. Most recently for my boiler. Mine is a tankless flat-looking effort affixed to the utility-room wall, which became really visible to me only through its failure (albeit not for the first or second time).

I found myself muttering obscenities through gritted teeth, giving the boiler a proper good dressing-down: 'You know full well what you're supposed to be doing – you do it beautifully for about three hours and then you miraculously forget *again*, you fucking . . .'

Later, while evanescing in the eternity of everythingness on my bed, I found myself getting annoyed, being swept away on the tide of irritating thoughts about my unreliable boiler.

When I was redelivered back into the room, the absurdity of this thought gave me pause to wonder: 'What about including the boiler in my little daily worship?' I don't mean building a shrine to it, but just by saying it a prayer it would become elevated to a place of deeper respect.

At the very least, it ought be given occasional honourable mention for preventing me from freezing to death.

Dear Boiler,

Thank you, from the bottom of my heart.

I am grateful for all the brains who had the persistence that I don't have to invent, improve and maintain you. Without you and those behind you tirelessly grafting away behind the scenes, nothing else would get done. All my hopes and dreams would fail, and life would be turned upside-down. Sorry for shouting at you earlier. I know nothing about how you work, and yet I rely on you to keep me alive – and still I have the gall to call *you* a cunt?

You see, it's because I've come to need you so badly. You are the beating heart of my home. And I use that as justification to hold you to an unreasonably high standard. Cards on the table, my frustration was really borne out of having to confront my own powerlessness in being unable to fix you.

Um . . . Amen?

The ancient Chinese philosopher Lao Tzu brilliantly cooked this one up for the *Tao Te Ching* while squatting in the forest:

When beauty is perceived,

Ugliness is created.

When people perceive good,

Evil is created.

Being and non-being create each other.

Difficult and easy support each other.

Long and short define each other.

High and low depend on each other.

Before and after follow each other.

God, to me, used to be no more than just a word, ensconced in a prayer that we were made to learn off. 'God!' was an expletive. It was an abstract symbol that conjured absolutely nothing in body and next to nothing to mind.

But once the benefits of practising simple beingness began to settle in, after a good eight months to a year of inner struggle, god became an experience, like being picked up by the scruff of the neck and dipped into a vat of love. An experience that needs no exchange of any information to begin understanding, no hope that some wilful, mysterious entity is in the right mood to treat you favourably. And oddly, attaching a word to it, like god, trips the simple circuitry of it.

Once, I watched out the living-room window as our child-hood cat, Pamela Anderson, carried her kittens one by one by the scruffs of their fragile little necks along our windowsill. She was bringing them in out of the cold. And it made for a shocking sight, these sleepy, helpless little kittens dangling there from their mother's befanged mouth. At first, my brain thought she was eating them.

I could yarn on and on in more and more words and meta-phors, and plenty more have, which I fear only casts more fog of mind over the profound simplicity of what practising medi-tation really is. In the end, once the storms of wild thought have been accepted and eventually subside, and you relax and let more go, it is simpler than doing anything else you can think of.

Because it is just attuning to emptiness, not in the absence of thoughts but in the absence of thoughts indulged. For me, discovering that sensation was realising that there is an enormous attic space above/basement space below my need to get anywhere or get anything done. Behind it all, behind all of the drama, we are the embodiment of this extraordinarily fulfilling emptiness/still-ness/godness, where nothing need be asked for, because (deep enough down), we know we are an expression of everything already. Sitting in quiet contemplation, a nice long meditation is the opposite of prayer, because it is not one entity communicating with another entity, it is simply being all entity all at once, because there's only one anyway.

So, my first religious experiences felt performative. And, para-doxically, my first performative experiences were religious. A profound suspension of self, combined with a powerful sensation of connectivity to others and the world around me.

When I was twelve, we put on a play for the parents entitled *Oliver with a Twist!*, the title dreamed up by our school's afore-mentioned headmaster/puppeteer, Des.

It was my first experience of treading the boards, and my first experience of generating laughter and applause from a crowd. Every night, I picked three audience members, got them up on stage, put them on their knees and made them pray: 'O Lord, bring me a horse! O Lord, bring me a horse!' Each time, more rhapsodically: 'O Lord, please bring me a horse!' There'd be a pause when I would look around and, disappointedly, still find no horse, only then to deliver the punchline: 'Well, he didn't bring us a horse, but he did deliver three fine asses.' And the crowd would roar! Hallelujah! Hosanna in the highest! A water-tight gag guaranteed to inspire a bellyful of connection every night as joy erupted like a volcano.

Playing Oliver at twelve years old in this play, and perhaps even delivering this specific gag, set the wheels of my condition-ing strongly in motion.

Merriam Webster's definition of 'operant conditioning' is this:

Conditioning in which the desired behaviour or increasingly closer approximations to it are followed by a rewarding or reinforcing stimulus.

Operant conditioning is a term popularised by an American psychologist called B.F. Skinner, to describe a method of learning to do with punishments and rewards. He theorised that our behaviour is not independently formed, but rather *completely* shaped by our environment through positive and negative stimuli. And therefore our free will is essentially an illusion. In fact, he went one step further and claimed that there is no such thing as an inner life. That everything we experience in our minds is a result of our external environments.

Famously, he demonstrated his operant conditioning by making pigeons perform simple moves inside of a Skinner box, a box that gave the pigeon simple instruction, like to peck or turn around, in order to receive a reward in the form of seed.

It is true that many of our choices are 'animal', in that they are about sustaining life and the avoidance of negative consequences. But it is also true that we are privy to many more layers of awareness, from which we have the ability to make decisions which surpass our base impulses.

That said, the thrill of getting that religious level of laughter and connection out of a crowd of people hugely conditioned me. It set me on a lifelong course of showing off professionally. I was the pigeon in the Skinner box, only showing far less restraint.

And the 'three fine asses' gag in *Oliver* was my baptism, then when I was fourteen, I received the Holy Communion and Confirmation all rolled into one.

Around then, over the course of about eighteen months, my mother, Maria, god preserve her, and I schlepped up to Dublin city a good few times on the train so that I could audition for a film called *Song for a Raggy Boy*. It was adapted from a book of the same name by Patrick Galvin, a man who had experienced some terrible examples of the aforementioned clerical abuses after being shipped off to a Catholic reformatory school when he was a little boy.

So, unsurprisingly, the nationwide open casting for this film, broadcast on children's daytime television, manifested hordes of little singing and dancing show-off twerps, with hopeful parents behind them carrying the bags.

Finally the final call took place in Lansdowne Rugby Football Clubhouse, which sits along the river Dodder in south Dublin. After many hours slumped against a mirrored wall, drinking vats of tea and eating too many bags of crisps, my name was called. I remember having the thought that we had put so much effort in, and now was my chance to make the most of it. I was ushered through by a clipboard-armed girl into the inner sanctum, where sat the almighty adjudicators behind a white-clothed table. The director, Aisling, casting director, Dorothy, and some other producer types who've long since been lost to the fog.

I was reading for the smartest and toughest boy of all, Liam, the leader, the one that the rest fall in behind. In the scene where Mr Franklin, the lay teacher, loses his temper with him for bullying another lad, and then he pushes and pushes him until eventually Liam lashes out and screams 'Fuck you!', back in the face of the only authority figure in the school he can trust.

So we read the scene. And then we read it again. And this time, when the emotional bit came, I gained a surprise sort of access to something very real inside myself. It felt like hitting the ejector button and an upward blast of wind lifting me clean off the ground. Up in the air, it was all snow blindness. My senses having yielded clean over to adrenaline. I felt reincarnated beyond my self into a being of pure light. And when my feet landed back down on the audition-room floor I was panting for breath, shaking, and wiping hot streaming tears off my cheeks. I blinked, looked around and collected myself, and saw Aisling, the director, smiling from ear to ear. And she, in turn, threw an encouraging nod over to Dorothy, who then wrote something down on a piece of paper.

The whole eighteen months before that, the butterflies had been jostling in the pit of my stomach like the grinding wheels of the train up to Dublin Heuston station. That entire time since the first call, I'd been harbouring a heavy anticipation. A hope that the day would be on my side, and now, it had all culminated in this magical, transformative moment.

And as I wiped away the tears, I was oscillating between a strange mix of exhilaration, confusion and *intense* embarrassment. Exhilaration that I had gone in and given it my all and held nothing back. Confusion because nothing like that had ever happened to me before. And intense embarrassment because I had just displayed a great deal of vulnerability in front of a bunch of strangers.

No emotional cloudburst the likes of this had ever occured. This complete abandon of self, through pretending?! Afterwards, as I walked out of there, I felt strangely certain that I'd got some part in it.

And, as the clipboard girl small-talked me back to the holding area, all I knew was that the vulnerability I had just shown provided ample justification for the woeful, awful feelings of embarrassment I was now feeling. Because I knew that what had been expressed, those very real emotions, were just what they were looking for. And as I walked over to Mam, the shame dissipated like a mist, and was absorbed by all the good feelings, as I eagerly shared with her how well I thought it had gone.

My teenage-headed interpretation of this event, however, began another set of interesting wheels grinding. Wheels which led to an embedded belief that would play out in me for years to come. And that belief was that real emotional vulnerability is *only* valuable as acting currency.

What I had learned to express in that audition room that afternoon ran completely contrary to the other set of social rules I'd already learned through my peer group: that accessing and expressing *real* emotional vulnerability was a sign of weakness, and best off hidden.

It wasn't until years later, and the discovery of this through practising some watchfulness, that I would come to understand how it was all well and good being vulnerable in front of an audience or a camera, shedding tears and expressing emotions that many wouldn't allow themselves to express, but this expressiveness was the very thing that contributed to *stymieing* my real-world emotional development.

Because the other set of social rules that governed the real world still reigned supreme. And, in honouring both sets of rules, this reinforced the belief in young Rob's mind that emotional fragility was something best kept within the parameters of performance. That to be *truly* vulnerable was to pretend.

O, gentle, pulsing Isness,

You are a wordless song.

How could I not have known you,

When you've been there all along?

Apart from my fellow-siblings, the other most wonderful thing about acting on *The Umbrella Academy* was that there were plenty of days off. And, on top of this, my character Klaus was a complete deadbeat, not remotely interested in appearing heroic or fighting crime, which resulted in me having to do to little to no stunt rehearsals. And all of this extra juicy leisure time meant that my meditation practice could resume, and resume it did with great gusto. In those six months, between January and July of 2018, I spent many, many, many hours conducting inner light experiments in my bedroom.

In the midst of all the insistent mind junk, the only tools at my disposal (which I had picked up from somewhere or other on the internet) were vagal breathing for relaxing the body, and the mantra for replacing the mind.

Our vagus nerves are a complex system of nerve fibres that roam around the body from the brainstem to the gut. They regulate breathing, heart rate, hormones and digestion. They are our brain's organ communication network. The Romans gave it the name 'vagus'. In latin, *vagus* means 'wandering', a word that shares its root with words like 'vague' and 'vagabond'.

Vagal breathing is to take long, slow, purposeful breaths.

This broadcasts a powerful signal to relax down through the branches and leaves of our autonomic nervous system through the vagus nerves. Vagal breathing switches awareness from the sympathetic to the parasympathetic nervous system, which is crucial for calming the body and removing the stress-chemical residue from any previous fight/flight responses brought on by worrying or environment. It's amazing how deep the body will go in just three or four conscious breaths.

Simple vagal breathing has been shown to have significantly positive effects. It rebalances the endocrine system, which regulates our hormone transmitters, rebalances blood pressure, and soothes symptoms of arthritis and chronic anxiety. Also, fascinatingly, it has been proven that *sounding out an exhale*, meaning exhaling while making a sound, and listening to that sound further positively stimulates the vagus nerves.

Breathing in big, holding for three or four, then letting it all go, bit by bit, really helped to reclaim focus beyond the noise of my mind so as to begin the love affair with it.

Slowly pulling air gently into my body, all the way down to the pelvic floor. Holding on to it for just a few seconds, letting focus winnow from brain to bum and back again. Before letting it all go and letting the body fall. A useful trick I learned starting off was to place my hands on my lower torso or lower back, and send my breath down to my hands as it came in. This stimulates the diaphragm, intercostal, abdominal and pelvic-floor muscles, and positively stimulates the vagus nerves. In that low hold, my body lets go of more needless surface tension, and the neural connections between my body and I are nourished.

Later, as a little variation, I used that vagal breath window at the start to say a prayer and thank my body. And to thank the oxygen that was permeating through it, giving it life.

After five or ten or however many breaths I needed to settle, next I'd do a nice bodyscan. Focussing down into the deep chasm of the body, beyond the jurisdiction of my thoughts. Taking a nice, slow tour of the grounds, to corners of the gardens I wouldn't typically go. Scanning around slowly begins building stronger neurological fluency between my body and mind by combing through the patches of sensory 'darkness' inside, on the way back to already established highways of light. Martyn Ford, the actor and professional fitness beefcake, told me when we were training that muscle growth is greatly dependent on how well one focusses the mind's eye into the muscle that one is exercising. The simple bodyscan works on the same principle.

I've heard it said that it is good to begin scanning the body from the outside (arms and legs) inwards first, to get you used to it, so that you are not hijacked or overwhelmed by any unpredicted feelings. Intuitively, you might feel this is right for you. Personally, I've found that lovingly leaning into the places where I am feeling the most a more nutritious pastime.

Now, at this stage of operations, when the body is rippling nice and low, cue the mindless mind-chatter!

The most useful tool at hand was the tool required for all of the unwanted self-talk: the mantra.

The mantra is like typical thinking, but in reverse. Instead of the thoughts coming towards you, you are sending them the other way.

The mantra is the central technique in the teaching of Maharishi Mahesh Yogi's Transcendental Meditation.

The word 'mantra' is based on the Sanskrit roots *man* (mind) and *trai* (liberation). It exists right where form and consciousness tug-o'-war, where flesh pulls at the spirit.

To employ a mantra is to repeat a phrase silently, using only the inner voice, so that you are presently speaking to yourself.

Repeating the phrase gently, over and over, over and over, like the rolling tide.

'Now, create an artificial wave … consciously add a new component … choose a single thought … and consciously set about

making that thought dominant ... Now each
wave is that same thought over and over
again ...'

Ram Dass, *Remember, Be Here Now*

The wave can be melodic or monotonal, ideally as long as it's a nice-feeling sound to repeat. A sound with broad, resonant vowel sounds and a pleasing rhythm conducive to promoting inner relaxation.

To repeat a mantra is to speak from the *present* heart to a surface mind which is typically gabbling on about the past or the future. And when a mantra is focussed on and gently repeated, one experiences near-instant cessation of the monkey mind – that one that slings handfuls of unwanted thoughts into your head unannounced. A mantra is just like laughing, because we also cannot think random thoughts and laugh at the same time.

The mantra was just the thing to help me to begin disentangling my sense of self from random thought patterns.

Throughout 2018, while making *The Umbrella Academy*, I began practising meditation by using the mantra *ohm mahne padme hum*. I still do for settling things down when my head is extra noisy. At first, *ohm mahne padme hum* had a habit of conceptualising itself in my mind's eye in all sorts of different ways. I let my imagination run off with *ohm mahne padme hum* like a dog with a string of sausages in its mouth. *Ohm mahne padme hum* appeared emblazoned on enormous billowing flags in the sunshine, or as giant chrome silver balloons, or emerging out of the darkness of a manhole cover to form swirling mandalas, like the way a production company's attention-seeking logo pops up at the start of the movie.

Ohm mahne padme hum as big brass bells ringing at the top of a Gothic church tower, or as a bald-headed monk with heavy mascara on who is super close and looking me right in the eye, and he barely whispers the phrase and I can see the cigarette stains on his teeth and the cold smoke of his breath. As pages flying out of a photocopier, or as flakes of crusty skin peeling off an ostrich's sunburnt leg. And so on and so on, you get the idea. In other words, my first instinct with a mantra was to put it to work creating stuff. To employ it as a kind of distraction technique by painting pictures with it in my imagination. To do something 'productive' with it. To use it like mental Lego bricks – which is fine, because that's where my head was at the time and that's what I needed to do.

In the initial struggle, when first confronting my own gauntlet of thoughts head-on, the mantra felt like nothing more than a rickety set of old windscreen wipers in the middle of a surging rainstorm. Mantra wipers wiping back and forth on the highest setting, making loud scrubbing noises on the glass, and only just about managing to deal with the downpour by keeping a small curved section of my windscreen semi-rainless and clear, so that I could just about see the line of the dark road out in front.

After six months, the mantra began to improve a little in efficacy, and gradually started settling down my thinking reflex. It gained in power. Slowly but surely, I began shifting the mantra wipers down a setting or two as the rainstorm began to subside.

This led to discovering a defogger switch (as he beats this windscreen analogy to death with a wet stick), which meant the capacity to see more and more of the road out in front of me. Further out into the evening, further than just my own lane. On a clear-headed night, nestled comfortably in a good bathing session on my bed, I could see the whole world whizzing by and the stars brightening up above. As the mantra helped me expand beyond my thoughts, my ability to see the world expanded too.

Maharishi Mahesh Yogi, the best-known exponent of Transcendental Meditation, suggested that once the mantra phrase has adequately replaced the choppy mind-chatter, to then begin repeating the mantra softer, and softer, and softer. To settle that dominant wave right down, that phrase that has disallowed all other mental activity, until the mantra itself is now barely registering on the heart-monitor screen of awareness. And then, the focus (you) becomes seriously signposted towards the emptiness all around the thingness – that which is there all by itself. The space of the rest of the monitor screen, and the machine the monitor is attached to, and the hospital bed it's sitting beside, and the sound of the birds and the traffic outside the hospital window: what is there in awareness in the absence of all of the activity of the individual self.

Thus, the mantra is a super-simple tool for restoring in us a fair degree of authority over a mind made incoherent through neglect. The raw grip of which leads many of us to conclude early on that practising stillness is pointless.

After silently repeating *ohm mahne padme hum* many thousands of times, it evolved. From just the thought of it into a kind of sacred feeling.

It turned into a lightsabered catalyst of calm, the silent utterance of which created a thunderbolt of connectivity between bodymind and me. Like lightning leaping out of the sky and forking down to touch the earth. And with no more need for any manhole covers or ostriches or monks to appear visually, conceptually, or otherwise.

With practice, the mantra became a function that began to bypass my mind altogether, like the quality of implicit mindlessness one experiences while riding a bicycle, only sitting very still.

Now, the final, and probably most crucial component of all when first approaching meditation/yoga/stretching/existing (which I learned in Bali, and was reminded of again in a yoga class in Portlaoise), is *ahimsa*.

Ahimsa is another ancient Sanskrit word, which roughly translates into English (I'm deeply suspicious of translations) as 'non-violence'. *Himsa* meaning 'violence', and the *a* prefix giving it its opposite meaning – which is a device English inherited from Sanskrit. Like how 'atypical' means the opposite of 'typical'. *Ahimsa* conveys the intention of universal love and compassion towards all things, beginning with yourself. *Ahimsa* means self-compassion.

I am unable to sit comfortably in the lotus position. The lotus position is the typical cross-legged sitting position associated with meditation, where the hips are open enough to allow the legs to lie flat in a pretzel shape in front of you on the floor. I had wrongly associated the lotus position with the concept of a 'successful and proper meditation', and would get frustrated and beat myself up and be critical towards myself for not being able to do it. I no longer subscribe to this notion.

The gates of blissfulness do not open exclusively for those with the 'correct' posture. Joy incarnate is not that interested in what shape your physical body is assuming. It's only interested in whether or not you're relaxed and comfortable enough.

This pose business put me off at the beginning because it made my body hurt. Trying to sit this way, cross-legged on the floor, made my knees sore and the left side of my back needly with pain. It was a kind of vanity on my part that I felt I needed to sit that way.

Recently, a blunt chiropractor/car mechanic named Chris took a look at me all stretched out on his slab and said, while chewing gum, 'Yeah, you sit a lot.' Too much sitting, ladies and gentleladies – it's the new smoking, apparently.

For me, I have quite a long, majestic back. And at the bottom of it, my little ass muscles don't pull their full weight in my posterior chain, the chain of muscles along the backside of the body. I currently fall shy of 'posterior dominance' because my glutes don't fire in the way that they should do (scuse me). So, historically, when sitting, bending over, getting out of a chair or doing just about anything, other muscles around my ass have had to overwork to compensate for their slacking neighbours. Namely, hamstrings, IT bands and lower back. This is a common enough problem, apparently. Many of us sit all day long.

God knows I spent enough time trying to sit comfortably pretzel-legged, trying to crowbar my body into that shape because I once saw a Buddhist monk do it on a postcard; but right now my hips can only do the lotus after *extensive* warming up. I spent too much of my youth sitting on chairs and couches.

Now, when practising stillfulness, I sit on cushions, a couch or the bed. The idea is to relieve the skeleton entirely of its obligation to support, protect, anchor and move. And not put extra strain on it by attempting to look like the monk clad in orange robes just before they poured the petrol over him. Feeling obliged to be able to sit that way flat on the floor was a roadblock, a hindrance to my practice, not a help.

For those of us whose bodies are more prone to sitting in lotus, it truly is a gift in meditation. In the rare times when my bottom half was warmed up enough to sit upright in lotus, the whole sensation of my lower body dissipated until I was a half-bodied man emerging out of the ground.

Once I was sitting in lotus on a large, smooth rock slanting down over the shores of Lake Ontario. I had my back to the city facing south, gazing across the still water at a skyline of apartment buildings shaped like a ship's sails in full mast. Sensationally, there was no difference between the rock and my folded legs. It was an experience which, I suppose, inspires that slightly irritating saying they have in Buddhism: 'Posture is meditation.'

Sitting flatly on your real seat in lotus supports the back in such a way that you no longer need to *maintain* the posture of uprightness. The hips maintain it for you with zero effort. Then, one can rest the bones fully and forget all about the body while still sitting bolt upright like a spring.

This is a game-changer. Because not having that ability makes those week-long meditation retreats hard on the body, I can tell you. I wish I could sit in lotus, but I can't yet and have had to let it go for now. But the art of listening to oneself closely in listenfulness guides the body from within by intuition, and ultimately tells you loud and clear what areas you need to work on to bring balance. After a certain point, when a quality enough range of motion was reached, the body began to intuit which parts needed more flexibility, and which parts more strength. There was no need to hire anyone to tell me. The message needed for balance became abundantly clear.

In the background, the quest for lotus and posterior dominance continues, but I no longer beat myself up about it. I'm hoping that, through strengthening and stretching, one day my stiff hips will plateau and from that point on, I will be able to sit down anywhere on this planet comfortably and be instantly rooted to the earth like a plant. Who knows, maybe in the next life.

A simple guide

‿

Here is a simple guide to begin voyaging into space.

Allow some time. You've been busy, running around talking lots of shite, so give yourself at least ten minutes to sit your ground. Set a timer if you'd like.

Sit up/lie down comfortably. Doesn't have to be cross-legged. Admission to the indoor vacation is not exclusive to those who can sit like Buddha.

Close your eyes.

Take at least a couple of minutes' worth of long, slow, loving vagal breaths. All the way down to the pelvic floor. Collect yourself, and get fully settled. Gently shake the obvious excess neurology out of the body.

Navigating towards relaxation is innate. Physical tension has just as identifiable a flavour as relaxation. Find it and get to know more about the corners of the body where it likes to reside (brows and lower right back are two hotspots for me). Then, let it drift away on the breeze of breath as best you can, and no rush. I find it helpful to approach meditation as a kind of unbodying experience, thinking of it as leaving my shell for a while like an overly adventurous hermit crab.

If/when the impulse to do something else intensifies, or mind-chatter appears and becomes frustrating and tediously distracting, don't try and rid yourself of it; instead, accept it. And gently meet it with your mantra. Why not try using the symbol ☀ as a mantra? Start by visualising that as a means of replacing the incessant newsreel. And then, after a little while, allow the eye to close until it can no longer be seen.

Let beingness echo silently from your heart through the rest of your form. Filling up your whole chest cavity and skull with pleasure.

Have a little faith and ignore any and all compulsion to judge how you think it's going or how it went. Either way – wonderfully or awfully – it's a roadblock to the practice. To delay all judgement, good or bad, for a period of time while learning the art of sitting still and taking a look is definitely to take a leap of faith, because it will likely include a period when you must ignore your own intuition to stop.

At that critical point, to keep meditating on is to welcome this overwhelming aversion fully, this static electric surge urging you to get up and leave stillness alone, and to note how this feeling is happening within the stillness all around it, which is giving it the context of its movement. Without the stillness and peace wrapped around it, we would have no idea how to cross-reference the severity of this fierce desire to stop. The struggle to pull myself away from peaceful stillness got choppier and choppier the further and further I swam out to sea. Wave after wave crashed down on me, trying to drive me back to shore. But just like in the sea, a little further out beyond the break, once you're floating in waters of greater depth, there is calmness.

And the rest, as they say, is present.

Dropped!

Down in the steerage hold,

For a dram of the spirit b'low

Duck!

While staggering down the scuff'd wood step,

To where the old casks roll and fleck,

From side to side and a

Clack!

As metal bands flash,

And rum bleeds out of the

Crack!

Soaking black all the wood'n scuff

And white by the heels of the

Dead!

Dragged by the nails of a few bare feet,

In the heart of the

Dark!

is a welcome rest from the gruelling heat ...

Pitfalls

Here are some unwanted things that happened as a direct result of practising meditation. Pretty much all of which could be classed as quarrels with my ego.

Embodying stillness offered a way of seeing the conditioned mind, and a way out of the conditioned mind, the shallowest of waters, which included such piranhas as overthinking and craving. A way out that felt like it had been lost. Or that I'd never had any need of before. This young conditioned mind with lots of distance between home and he, lots of expensive dinners and flights he wasn't paying for, lots of casual lovers (when he was single, mostly), and a fair whack of romantic dysfunction (when he wasn't single, frequently). All repressed beneath a pastry layer of self that told me that I was just fine. I mean, 'Look how well things are going.'

And with no way out of that conditioned mind, other than ways that cost money or damaged the organs over time, looking back it felt like my life was being only fractionally lived. So I experienced initial shrinkages of character in between these new expansions.

My first instinct after finding pleasurable emptiness was to just stay in there. In the deeper, more euphoric, less vocal consciousness of my self. Stay cosited in there, like a baby, suck-ling endlessly from emptiness's teat. This was in the infancy of my practice.

Having found this unexplored, previously unnoticed terri-tory inside, and even layers of dream consciousness that were better for hallucinations than any psychedelic I'd ever taken, suddenly in my early thirties I thought, 'Well, there must be lots more in here that I have so far missed.' And so being down/up there as an excuse for being somewhere other than the material world felt wholly justified. This was the tricky high-wire walk with the practice, at first, and I definitely fell on the far side of the rope.

I was using meditation as a form of escape, like a drug, using meditation as a way to feel better about myself, like a crutch. Using meditation as a justification for being lazy, like a lazy bastard. Using meditation as a hurdy-gurdy multicoloured hallucinatory carnival ride. Using meditation as a form of sensualism. When I was thinking up titles for this book one that popped out was 'A Sensualist's Guide to Meditation', which made me laugh, which means there must be some truth to it.

Also, as the expanding spaciousness within was putting a newer, larger, shape on things. My ego took advantage of this, as something that it could tell was of benefit to us. Despite the fact that my ego had fought the practice, and the earning of said spa-ciousness, every step of the way. I cringe in admitting uttering some very boastful, very stupid statements out loud around the 2018/19ish mark to do with the practising of meditaaaaaaaaaaation. A choice one being something I said to my pal Ronnie, without irony in my kitchen in London: 'You know, some evenings, I can literally go for hours not thinking.' What a moron, and what a lie too. Another choice statement, when correcting another actor on

Umbrella, I said, 'Enlightenment's not hard. Not that hard at all.' This is, I assume, a strange pitfall that occurs. That when any bit of genuine spaciousness is earned within, the ego, the part of us that wants everything to be OK but sometimes worries too much, attempts to reassert its authority over that new space and use it as a means to feel superior over others. And the ego's activity, the surface frothing of the mind, is compelling because it is so strongly connected to emotions.

Or at least it is in my case. I think it is mainly this pitfall that leads some early practitioners to come across like the afore-mentioned 'prats'. Because it is an oppressive move to others, to throw around such egoic statements, the subtext of which is declaring and being received as, 'I am better than you.'

Especially when speaking about something as fundamental and intimate as how we relate to our inner selves.

Another interesting one that occurred along the road, and something that I had to become more conscious of, was this occasional state of complete unwanted mindlessness brought on by practising meditation, in situations when I really needed my mind to function. This would mainly occur once I'd had a nice creamy frollick in the foam of floatiness, and was then immediately thrust into a very social, very vocal situation.

I remember the car ride from the hotel around the corner to the red carpet for the premiere of the movie *Mortal Engines* in Los Angeles, wearing this ridiculous black suit dripping in studded dia-monds, wherein I'd intentionally gone deep into a meditative state just to see what would happen. 'To go into so intensely stimulating an environment, with its incredibly bright lights and shiny smiling people, and hordes of journalists and photographers, with the full clarity of beingness would be interesting,' I thought to myself. But the problem was when I stepped out of the darkness and walked onto that big red carpet – *flash! flash! flash!* – my head was *very* much still in the car. Because I had neglected to reset myself afterwards by setting a new intention, a new direction, and getting my head back 'in the game', as it were. So there were journalists asking me all these questions about the movie, and I was offering replies like, 'You know, I don't think I know how to answer that question.' It was absurd, and serves as a reminder just how far away inside one's own consciousness one can go. What distances one can travel in a relatively short time.

Another thing that I believe my ego (in the form of many-headed thinking) did was get a little confused, and begin to tell me that its own activity was bad. I experienced a form of ego-denial, and began to passively reject the thinking part of myself. If a thought emerged of its own accord it was, by definition, dirty, and ought be treated like some sort of unwanted foreign body and cast out. My ego was behaving like a two-headed snake fighting itself for the same food.

This happened slowly and subtly, and for a while, I'd be trying to 'apply techniques' over the top of it. Techniques for whenever I caught myself thinking. Like repeating a mantra or quickly redirecting my focus out of my skull and down to my feet or something, which were pointless wastes of energy. These were just more subtle versions of me trying to get my thoughts in a chokehold again, as opposed to just simply seeing it all as another feature of the present landscape, before letting it pass by my mind's window. There was this kind of fundamental rejection of a significant part of myself, the very opposite of warm-hearted *ahimsa* acceptance.

And – to my credit, in fairness – it got to where if it did happen and I automatically applied my 'stop thinking' technique, it would make me expel air from my nostrils in a little chuckle at this absurd habit I had picked up, like avoiding walking on the cracks of the pavement. I think the conundrum is that when the objective of practising nomindness is believed to be 'ceasing all thinking' or 'switching one's mind off', then one naturally begins to start having a lower opinion of natural thinking.

And when thinking began to cause this subtle sense of guilt in me, this strange feeling of original sin whenever a thought popped across my palette, it signified the beginning of a blue period of over-feeling.

Over-feeling was another interesting and unexpected side effect of meditation.

Having spent some substantial time permitting and encouraging all the unconscious stuff up to the foreground of awareness, it now meant that emotions began turning up more regularly of their own accord. Like unwanted pigeons on my stoop. I experienced a period of indulgence during which I got into the mindset that it was somehow my duty to acknowledge how I was feeling *all* of the time. And this is perhaps another form of ego distortion. My pal Larry once referred to his teenage self as 'ambi-centric', by which he meant that there was pride there – oh yeah, baby, there was – but it was turned inwards, not outwards. So Larry's ego had him tricked into believing that what he was feeling was not pride. That it was something else. And when he realised this, that the compulsion that drove him to hold himself back and be quieter in social settings was the same feeling that drove others to be louder and more cocksure, it was like a lightbulb switching on inside his head. And now this next bit is conjecture on my part, but this probably made it easier for him to have compassion for and get on with other, louder people.

As compassion and joy in me grew, so did my propensity to feel sorrow. There were days when I felt as though the practice of meditation, looking at emotions big and small, was really changing me for the worse.

I'd never had *whole* days cloaked in raw sadness before. *As Gaeilge* (in the Irish language) when it comes to relating to our emotions, the preposition 'on' is employed. *Tá brón orm* literally translates as 'there is a sorrow on me'. And that is what this sorrow felt like, that meditation had thrown a blanket over me – thankfully along with enough of an appetite to be right there and keep going with what I was feeling and not run away from it.

And I was confused, because here I was supposed to be gaining greater space and clarity around my emotional life, but it felt like it was having the complete opposite effect. That it was plunging my head down the U-bend of a toilet.

'I expected a liberation from my feelings, not an intensification – this feels fucking pointless!' I thought, while immediately trying to get that thought into a headlock.

And because my sorrow intensified, it got to the point where it was passively keeping me from going fully back there altogether. Kept me from allowing real emotion in, or 'on'. So, for a while, I had a kind of pretend meditation going on. Where I would 'marinate my attention', as the spiritual teacher Mooji says, in unchanging being, but only up to a point. Beyond which was a depth my mind refused to allow us to go. Meditation was demoted to a pastime I went back to here and there, for ten minutes or so windows on the couch or bed, as opposed to allowing change to flow and permitting myself to become more spatial all the live-long day.

And then there was this other strange, observable pitfall that occurred, where I began to use a form of meditation as a kind of escape hatch. Part of the transformation meant that, whenever I was out in the world, I was more eager to tune in through my senses. Tune in to the environment around me through what I could hear, feel, smell, etc. Allowing myself to fully marinate in my surroundings, eyes open or closed, so that I could become more absorbent, and absorb more of the world's texture, and therefore be enriched to a greater degree by the experience of being in that place.

Like permitting my gaze to drift slowly over many individual objects. Dwelling on the young acorns in that funny-coloured tree, the large orange parasol shading the outdoor seating with the word 'WIGGLE' printed on it, or that yield sign over which someone had graffitied the words 'Hell yeah!' And the smells of coffee and frying food wafting across the open square. Allowing more time to get out of my own way, so that I could fall more deeply in love. But somewhere along the road, unexpectedly, I began using this new instinct to be fully (with)in my environment as a kind of escape hatch. Tuning in to my environs to escape what was emotionally really going on. For example, falling into my environment if an air of tension arose between my girlfriend and I. So that no longer was I falling in love with my environment but fleeing towards it. And then this new-found appetite for the world, this exciting desire to suspend my individual self for a while in places I'd never been, felt corrupted.

I remember walking down a sunlit, narrow cobbled street with my girlfriend, and there was a moment of tension between us, which put our footsteps out of sync and sent us drifting away from one another. And as we walked out onto the beautiful enclosed plaza, the next thought that came in was, 'Oh, look at the veneer on that lovely old apartment building. With its wrought-iron girded balconettes glinting in the sun and the pastel-coloured stone.' But along with this thought came the feeling that I was a complete clown. A coward who was really running away from his current feelings and sticking his head in the sand, and hoping in vain that the unwanted tension would simply go away on its own. Stillness/spaciousness/contentment/godlove, when starting off learning how to embody it, provides obstacles for itself. As old habits are shaken off, new ones can crop up. Or perhaps they are the same habits as always but now they're more visible. Or they've disguised themselves in new masks. This is why meditation feels comparable to something like LSD or a loaded handgun. It's an incredibly powerful thing, and as it unfolds, it can lead you down painful dead-ends if you don't navigate properly as you go.

Luckily, the simple guiding principle remains the same: an ever-present coastal lighthouse to keep the ship consistently on course, and that is *ahimsa*.

Walking along on those beautiful cobbled streets avoiding resolving some tension or other with my girlfriend was a moment that benefitted from my practice of *ahimsa*, the practice of self-compassion. Because it meant being able to have greater compassion for her, and not beating myself up too much for occasionally feeling like a scared little clown.

Kaboom

❧

The next thing that happened was an explosion in my solar plexus, brought on by a wiry Italian gentleman with locs down past his bum and some Tibetan singing bowls.

It was August 2018, and principle photography for season one of *Umbrella* was finished. We were all knackered, as the baton was handed off to the post-production team in Los Angeles, who, guided by overlord uncle Steve Blackman, would spend the next year fine-tuning the cut and completing complicated VFX shots involving a waistcoated chimpanzee.

After a very emotionally challenging first season, exploring Klaus's many dysfunctions, I was eager to get back to exploring my own.

I decided to go away on my holidays. I was eager to go somewhere meditation-y, to mingle with other souls making similar inroads into themselves, and sleep with every last one of them. No, my hope was that visiting the island of Bali, in Indonesia, would help grow my fledgling practice, which so far had just been me on my own by myself in a darkened bedroom. I was hungry to learn new means of remaining for more prolonged periods of time loitering in the lushness of lifeness undisturbed.

Going to Bali was a mission of sorts. A mission I should prob-ably have shared in advance with the friends I was going with. For the first vacation in my whole life, just going away to unwind and socialise and sight-see and party and drink and chat shit and wake up in the hot morning sun hungover only to do it all over again felt like a complete waste of time. Because it would have meant being in a very special place for such a finite amount of time and *not* being present, whether sitting still or no.

Bali is an environment that supports and encourages the frag-ile new practices of many, which require sustained periods of naval-gazing. It offered a kind of protection, one that I was cau-tious not to undermine. A world that wasn't really known to me nearer where I'm from, outside of a full-blown retreat (which comes later).

At this point, if you asked me, intellectually I might have told you that practising meditation is to become less rigid and more natural, but the truth was that the initial change that was happen-ing inside me was also painful.

I remember the first day arriving at the entrance of our big posh villa, just as evening was falling. And from inside the gates there was an eruption of group laughter and the clinking of glass bottles.

And I thought, 'Oh shit, I can't be doing this. I am in a very different mood to these people. I am here for forty nights in the desert, not to play beer pong.'

We'd all flown in from different worlds, different parts of the globe. And two of my five new roomies were friends of friends, people I hadn't even met yet.

One of our party was a woman I'd been seeing, who had flown to Bali and met me there. No doubt she was expecting a fun party time, the likes of which we'd already been having. But when she arrived, she was met with a very different me than the one she'd known.

I remember seeing footage of myself on her camcorder, emerging out of the mouth of an enormous Balinese cave with jagged teeth by the side of a country road. And to describe my default expression in the footage as resting bitch face would be an understatement. I was miserable-looking. Like someone had turned my clown upside down.

In Bali, all the property entrances have little gods protecting the gates. Fiersome warriors with their tongues stuck out, and their pupils dilated, to suggest that they are in a higher state of awareness. On that first night, rolling my suitcase through the gates of the villa, with its beautiful swimming pool, staff members milling around, and meticulously manicured gardens with Jurassic-leafed exotic plants, I was unable, or perhaps unwilling, to access the well-practised social part of myself.

Coping with the challenge of falling in step with this new group felt beyond me. So I kind of rejected their needs because I thought, 'To chip away at this social coalface here would be to "betray my personal mission" of getting to know more about myself,' or something.

I naively believed that to join in with the others meant being pushed further away from learning wisdoms that could only be found in the deepest of quiet. In other words, the vibe I was putting out on that holiday wasn't exactly the most friendly.

My fellow holidaymakers couldn't help noticing my refusal to join in, probably more so than I did. It gave rise to a strange, quietly broken atmosphere in the villa. None of us had thought to meet and get to know each other, even via a messaging app, in advance of moving in together.

After a few days, factions of us split off into our different groups and spent our days going our separate ways. Some to the beach, and others (me) to yoga/meditation /sound-healing classes, that type of thing.

Funny how things go backwards when you think they're going forwards. Or you don't realise it, but forwards feels necessarily like backwards for a time. As real love and compassion for myself was growing, it made me selfish. Made me recoil from the obligation of having to keep up the bare minimum of my side of the bargain.

This was symptomatic of my early days in the practice. All the euphoric transformation and discovery inward shut me down when I felt I had to be outward. And in Bali, feeling obliged to be present for every single footstep left me, for the first time since I was a teenager, feeling guarded and hesitant and uncomfortable around other people. I didn't like the way that jacket fit, but felt compelled to wear it. The others in my group were doing what comes *au naturel* in a group of young adults: drinking, carousing and generally being all chats in efforts to connect and make new friends and have a good time. But I indulged in my feeling of revulsion towards all that, a revulsion that was not communicated verbally. This experience could be likened to my first day at playschool in Mrs Whelan's class, only this time, by the end of my first day I still wasn't happy. Five years old and I still remember the abject terror, of peering in through the glass front doors of Mrs Whelan's Montessori playschool over the road, and seeing 25-odd children all covered in paint and bouncing off the walls like chimpanzees. And my mother, holding me by the hand and geeing me up with encouraging words in my ear, as she coaxed me inside while making pleasantries with Mrs Whelan. And as I watched her leave, with my face pinned up against the glass doors, I cried at the Shakespearean levels of betrayal. Abandoned by my own mother. Then later, at the end of the first day when Mam came back, I cried again. But this time at the Shakespearean betrayal of being torn away from all my new friends. I mean, sure, Bali was spectacularly scenic and stunning and vibrating with life, and I vibrated along with it in the giddy heights of landing in a brand-new place, but behind all that a subtle war had begun. A war with myself.

By casting myself out of the usual social carry-on, and trying to remain ever present, it amounted to feeling like I was lost in a kind of fog.

This had happened once before. I was in my mid-twenties, and wasn't yet ready to understand what was happening.

I went scuba diving in Cabo San Lucas, Mexico. I'd made some extra cash-in-hand by hand-signing some memorabilia cards for a film called *The Mortal Instruments: City of Bones*, where I played Simon, the friend-zoned corner of a supernatural love triangle. These memorabilia cards are like Top Trump cards of yourself that you sign and which get the undershorts of collector fans damp.

So I decided to blow the whole wad on an outdoorsy vacation. Down I flew on my Toblerone from Los Angeles, USA, to Cabo San Lucas, Mexico.

I ended up spending whole entire days there wandering alone by myself, around the beachside resort and the harbour-side promenades. I was without human company for far longer than I had spent in years probably, and I felt existentially lost in the heavy static of self-critical thinking. The streets of Cabo were all bright lights, happy hours, 600lb marlin freshly harpooned and hanging by the tail. People doing shots off each other on the bar, the possibility of new friends to charm, promiscuous sex to (re)confirm my status as an attractive man, but pickings were slim. Among the other holidaymakers, I found the atmosphere in Cabo jarringly unfriendly. It was mostly closed-off American couples and groups who found it strange if you talked to them with no seeming agenda. The only warmth and friendliness came in the form of Mexican hospitality. I couldn't shake the feeling that I was supposed to be somewhere else doing something else. By the end of the trip, I felt like half a person, if not less. Because I'd spent so much of my life situating my sense of self, my value, in the times when I was colliding with other people. So when I was left on my own for such a long stretch of time, all my sense of self, my confidence fell away, like the skin of a cadaver that had fallen off the back of a galloping horse and been left to dry out in the hot Mexican sunshine. I was consumed by doubt. To the point where I felt so inhibited when I got back to Los Angeles, I was reluctant to risk even saying hello to another human being across a shop counter.

The only moment of connection to myself that lingers from that trip to Cabo was when I was on an endless white-sand beach reading John Steinbeck's *The Pearl*.

Only by the end of the tale had I worked it out that Kino, Steinbeck's hero fisherman who dives down and finds the coveted pearl, dives the very same stretch of coast that I was lying on. Over my right shoulder, I could see the same hazy outline of jagged mountains before the town of La Paz, where he attempts to escape with his wife and baby, with pearl-hungry bounty hunters hot on their trail. Armed with no prior knowledge whatsoever, I found myself reading *The Pearl* in exactly the spot where it was set. When I realised this, it felt like a drink of fresh water in an ocean of salt. Like sitting in the universe's cupped hand. I whooped and cheered and hollered for joy! And no one heard me, except the Pacific tide, which has no memory anyway. And I thanked my inner child for having had the curiosity to read books early on, so that no matter where on the planet I roamed, I could always taste delicious connection just by opening a good book.

In Bali, perhaps partly down to playing Klaus, it was right at the height of that gloomy overfeeling phase, where I felt obliged to feel every single emotion to the max. There was no choice in it, because it was just where I was.

I spent the days buzzing from A to B around the bustling Bali streets on a moped in *very* loose-flowing, brightly coloured floral pants.

Chugging past endless fields of long grass all honking and squawking with toads. Speed-wobbling in slipstreams of lorries roaring past on cross-country highways. Cruising through dense, wet forests, whose canopies overhead were filled with platoons of white-haired long-tailed monkeys. One day, the monkeys laid siege to the promenade of local shops directly across from their forest. As we zoomed around the corner, we drove right into hordes of them fleeing in all directions carrying packs of cigarettes, chocolate bars and knock-off Louis Vuitton suitcases. All the shopkeepers were in hot pursuit trying to recover some of their stock. And then one of the shopkeepers let off a big red smoke bomb to deter the monkey invasion, and the smoke engulfed the entire street.

I drove out to the village of Bedulu to visit the famous temple of Goa Gajah, built about 1,100 years ago.

The temple survived because in the fourteenth century, as the Javanese were invading from the west, the last king of the

Pejeng kingdom, King Śri Astasura Ratna Bumi Banten, declared that the whole temple of Goa Gajah be buried and hidden from the invaders by putting a rice field over the top of it. And it remained that way until 1923 when, after an enormous earthquake, the rice field was displaced enough for a Dutch East Indies official to report finding a large statue of Ganesha there. After that, it took nearly three decades of excavation, and still to this day substantial parts of it remain underground.

You may only gain entry if a) you're wearing the correct ceremonial sarong, and b) you're not menstruating.

Water babbles down the valley's ravines into Gandhara (big fat) Buddha-shaped ponds, and trickles out of the still pools over the twisting roots of sacred trees growing up and over everything. Showing me around was Gade, a Hindu priest who also worked as a guide at the temple to make some extra booze and gambling money (joke).

Just before we got to the Elephant Cave, we stopped off to absorb a spectacular stone fountain called the Bathing Temple, where the water flows in via seven statues of female figures (six now, one was destroyed by an earthquake) all standing in a row. Each statue contributes her water into the central pool via her *manipura* or solar plexus chakra, meaning the energy centre on the human body that sits in the middle of the torso. Gade explained to me the ritual concerned with this bathing temple:

If there is something going on in your life that you would like to change – perhaps a habit you'd like to part with or a relationship that has ended in all but name – you identify it, get it clear in your mind, and then you walk barefoot into the water. While there, feeling its cool alertness on your skin, you wash your hands, your feet and your face. And then you realise the possibility in continuing to live happily without this thing in your life. And you make a pledge to embrace the abundance of life without it. Then you are baptised and reborn, with a new mission and new possibility, to lead a life in the absence of this thing you are letting go. I pledged to smoke less; it didn't work.

As Gade was explaining all this to me, there was lots of splashing and squeaking and giggling coming from inside the central pond. It was some loud American and Italian tourists who had waded in there to take loads of selfies. I asked him, 'Doesn't this strike you as profane? Disrespectful of this special place? Annoying that these obnoxious people come here and treat this place like Disneyland?' And he replied, 'No.' Well . . . alright then. 'They are just as they are,' he continued. 'Why expect something else from them?'

The Elephant Cave was jaw-dropping, quite literally. It stands exactly as it was over a thousand years ago. It is called such either because of the ancient Ganesha statue inside or because it sits at the concurrence of two rivers, one being the Pentanu River, once known as the Elephant River.

The mouth of the cave is the mouth of a fiersome warrior. He looks like a dragon on ecstasy.

Just like the little gods that protect the entranceways, his eyes are fiercely dilated. And carved around this open-mouthed face, like billowing clouds of rock, is a nebulous forest.

Peeking out from this nebulous forest hairdo are different animals, but only very subtly. Gade had to point them out. A tiger, a monkey, a bat, an elephant, a pig. Just barely, the snouts and eyes of these animal figures peer out, some baring their teeth or tusks, their bodies wholly hidden.

Gade pointed up at the forest around the warrior's head. 'What do you see, brother? Tell me what you see.'

'Hmm . . .' I faltered. 'Um, animals . . . That we are all god? All aspects of the same . . .' But he was already smiling and shaking his head. He tapped his temple, and then he tapped my temple.

'It is the unconscious mind, brother. Anger, fear, greed, jealousy, lust, hatred, avoidance, and so on. In this life, one must learn to control their animals, *nicely*.'

On the word 'nicely', he smiled warmly. These animals were visual metaphors for the different emotions all of us warriors experience as we pass through this state called human being.

This cave is a thousand-year-old guide on how to correctly identify and name difficult emotions. It is a human being's emotional instruction manual of sorts, simple enough for children to understand, and it serves as a reminder to every soul who walks through its mouth to remember that *all* of us, at different times, encounter dangerous animals in our forest.

These emotions, just like *as Gaeilge*, can sit on the back of us for a while, and therefore are essentially separate to us. It is the opposite in the English language where to describe the experience of the emotion, you become the emotion, 'I *am* happy' or 'I *am* sad.'

And the job of discerning a fulfilled life is first to be able to see them, so that you can begin to control them, nicely. I absolutely love that. Because encoded in it is the important connotation of making inner change through self-love, not through self-cruelty. Through 'I am nice. I am changing.' Not through 'I am·not good enough. I must change.' It is to understand our true position in the forest of the unconscious mind as the master. And to understand that we have a choice whether to be a malevolent or benevolent one.

Coming away, I felt enriched by such a simple yet universal analogy. And also couldn't help feeling a little short-changed by the instruction manual we'd been given growing up.

In these brief 1,100 years, the human experience has not changed. Our animals are still in the forest and that's the way it is. But by getting to know them, by familiarising ourselves with their tracks, where they hunt, where they sleep, what they feed on, then perhaps we can even come to love them. So that whatever hour of the night, we can always go for a nice, long relaxing stroll through the forest.

Now, before moving on to this next bit, I must first describe to you what I mean when I use the word 'shakti'. Shakti is a word derived from Sanskrit, and is used to describe a force of energy that permeates the whole universe.

Traditionally in Hinduism, shakti energy is depicted as many different goddesses, and the Kundalini snake is also a symbol of shakti energy. The Kundalini serpent coiled or slithering up the spine. Shakti is the energy of the universe, which can enter our bodies at the base and 'slither' its way upwards through the spinal column and out along the branches of our nervous system.

Shakti is an intelligent, primordial, flirtatious, creative/ destructive force. The Taoists called this energy *xi* in 500 BC. In India, the energy has also been known as *prana*. Pranayama is the practice of tapping into *prana*, to utilise it for a better quality of life. In Japan, this energy is known as *ki*. In Hawaii, it's called *mana*. In ancient Egypt they referred to it as *ka*, and around my way growing up they called it 'the holy ghost'.

If the Taoists are right, it is the same force that gives the animation of life to all form.

The ancient Egyptians also believed this, that a person's *ka* was the element that made them an alive thing as opposed to a not-alive thing. It was the thing they were most concerned about keeping nourished after mortal death.

Shakti is a good word though. Shakti, shakti. It has been adorned and suffocated by many words and symbols, and personified into many deities. When the pathways in the body become open, it becomes possible to draw on more of this energy to appear, and not in the form of how one thinks god looks in their mind's eye, but in the form of a very physical experience. An extremely pleasurable sensation, like bolts of cheeky lightning frolicking upwards through you.

I also believe that shakti, guided by a practised inner focus, has the power to heal.

'Where focus goes, blood flows.'

Wim Hof

In 2007, Wim Hof ran a marathon in the Arctic. He sustained 'extensive necrosis of the foot' from exposure to the cold. Necrosis is the localised death of living cell tissue most commonly caused by decreased oxygen and/or intense amounts of inflammation. On verywellhealth.com, a peer-reviewed medical practitioners' website it says: 'There are no self-treatments for necrosis, and you should not attempt to treat it at home.'

Wim's doctor's prognosis was that the likelihood he would keep his foot was minimal, so, rejecting an amputation procedure, he was prescribed a cornucopia of pharmaceutical pills. Likely a generous variety of non-steroidal anti-inflammatories, bisphosphonates and platelet aggregation inhibitors.

Wim rejected that prescription and instead chose to sit with the dead foot for hours per day, and let his 'inner fire', as he calls the shakti, flow into it. He spent weeks sitting in the shakti, sending his inner fire cascading into his dead foot. Gradually, it began to improve. It started showing meagre signs of life, and then after three months, it was fully healed.

Dr Joe Dispenza is a chiropractic doctor and *New York Times* bestselling author. In 1986, while bike-racing in a triathlon, he broke six vertebrae when he was hit by a Ford Bronco going at 50 miles per hour. It was a terrible mess. The prognosis was that without surgery, he would never walk again. Over the following ten weeks, he lay face down, marinating in the shakti.

'I believe that there's an intelligence, an invisible consciousness, within each of us that's the giver of life. It supports, maintains, protects and heals us every moment. It creates almost 100 trillion specialized cells (starting from only 2), it keeps our hearts beating hundreds of thousands of times per day, and it can organize hundreds of thousands of chemical reactions in a single cell in every second – among many other amazing functions. I reasoned at the time that if this intelligence was real and if it willfully, mindfully and lovingly demonstrated such amazing abilities, maybe I could take my attention off my external world and begin to go within and connect with it – developing a relationship with it.'

Dr Joe Dispenza

Using positive visualisation, and connecting deeply with his inner light, just nine and a half weeks after the accident, Dr Joe had fixed his spinal injury. Ten weeks later he was back seeing patients. If he had acquiesced to the most cutting-edge surgical solution, he would now have a huge metal rod in his back.

So, it stands to reason that allowing the focus to drift around the body to see what light it can find is a little worthwhile, just for its own sake.

Now, folks, I am no medical practitioner. Nor should any of this be interpreted as actual medical advice. But I believe, having experienced its joyousness for myself, and having discovered plenty of evidence to indicate it, that the shakti has an intriguingly powerful healing effect.

It was nearly my final day in Bali. And I went for the first time to what was being billed as a 'sound-healing class'. Even by my standards it sounded a bit wishy-washy, but I thought, 'Sure, fuck it, why not. What's the worst that could happen? Sounds relaxing. Little to no movement required, and at the worst, I might get a sweet nap out of it.'

The light-filled, high-ceilinged wooden room was generously sized, and we the student body took up the entire floor's worth of space. The sound of water flowing into water chuffled away somewhere at the back of the room, like in a lot of places in Bali, where they appreciate the value of flexible energy to human happiness. The playful sounds of it, the soothing feeling of it, nicely complementing all of the solid things. We, the sound recipients, sat facing a big gorgeous wall of glass which looked onto a rainforest's worth of fat-leafed tropical plants.

Once I'd found my spot, I noticed the teacher. A tanned, wiry man with enormous blue eyes and very long, seasoned locs of hair. He was sitting in front of the glass and quietly surrounding himself with a neat array of tuning forks, triangles, and a panoply of Tibetan singing bowls – all within tapping distance.

Once settled, he implored us in a dramatically Italian fashion to simply do only one thing: whenever we got naturally lost in thought, the thing to remember was to notice it and let it go, so as to tune right back into the sounds that he was making. That was it.

I sat pretzel-legged and closed my eyes.

He began the class with the percussion instruments that surrounded him. Then, after a healthy warm-up of dinging and gonging, he got up and began moving through the student body, and orbiting the resonating bowls around our bodies in close-up.

With Tibetan singing bowls, each bowl size correlates to a different chakra energy centre in the body. 'Chakra energy centre' meaning the little nerve bundles that we have, which gather along central points, and run from the bottom floor up to the top of the head. The smaller, higher-pitched bowls resonate at the frequencies of chakras that are higher up, like the throat and the 'third eye' chakra in the forehead. And the larger, lower-resonating bowls correlate in frequency with the chakra centres lower down, like the bowel or the solar plexus.

When he began walking around the room it was with the smallest bowls, and then he worked his way downwards. And it was interesting because he paid me next to no attention up until the point when he was holding a larger-sized singing bowl, one which was definitely correlating with the chakra in my solar plexus. The solar plexus is in our upper belly, right below the chest. It is two bundles of nerve fibres, or ganglia, which intertwine and then go past each other in the central abdomen.

As he closed in on me with this bowl, every molecule in my body began to vibrate, tears began to well, my breathing got heavy, and then something large in my solar plexus unclogged and dislodged so dramatically that it knocked me clean off my seat.

It felt like the inner parallel of the satisfaction you get from unclogging a stubborn drain with a plunger, and then seeing the water running smoothly down the hole. Only now multiply that feeling by a thousand. My whole body erupted upwards from the insides out, and the steaming tears came rushing like Old

Faithful, the thermal geyser which inspired the creation of the world's first national conservation area, Yellowstone Park.

It was like the removal of a thorn that had become wedged so deep that I had forgotten it was there. I had definitely forgotten what it felt like to be without it.

After quickly passing this huge emotional stool, I sobbed uncontrollably on the sprung wooden floor, face heaving against the yoga mat, and couldn't stop for about half an hour.

Crying is interesting. I've done a lot of it for money.

When something gets in our eye, the eye waters itself with what are called 'reflex tears' to void out the unwelcome intruder. When the eye moistens itself on the daily, those are called 'basal tears'. But then when we *cry* cry tears, tears of emotion, our tears are of a very different chemical composition. When the centre cannot hold and we reach that critical point – in either direction, sorrow or joy – these are called 'psychic tears'.

Crying retention – restraining oneself from crying – has been proven to be bad for our health. It contributes to stress, elevated blood pressure and heart disease. But when we let go and cry as a result of stress, the tears contain the stress hormone cortisol, and leucine enkephalin, a natural opioid that the body releases when under stress.

Cortisol is part of our body's chemical threat response: it helps to kick us into fight/flight/freeze mode, which takes its toll. Chronic low-level stress, i.e. continuous unrelenting stress, impairs our health badly over time.

When a body is in survival mode too frequently, with not enough chance to fully calm down, it corrodes its function and manifests in all sorts of ways. High blood pressure, suppressed immune response, artery clogging, ulcers, imbalances in the brain that can lead to depression, anxiety, addiction, gut issues, skin issues and the rest.

The link between the release of psychic tears and the release of endorphins and oxytocin in our bodies has been proven, which promote homeostasis (balance) and improves our mood.

When I finally collected myself off the floor of that sound-healing class, everybody else had gone. Even the wiry Italian teacher. I'd been lying there long enough for the whole student body to vacate the room, and for him to have packed up his whole one-man circus and got on with his afternoon. They all just politely left me there in that big wooden room with all the fat-leafed tropical plants. It was pure wet joy, and all I remember thinking was nothing.

Afterwards, I lay outside in a patch of sunny grass, and felt such a lightness of being that it would've been no surprise had I floated off up into the cloudless blue sky.

Only after this profound experience, and not before, did I possess the ability to summon the shakti force into my body. Once channels were open enough, a session of reclining back regally into restfulness became like ejaculating backwards up inside myself. Like fizzing liquid joy flowing through my veins, and just like water when the current is strong, it rushed over and under and right through everything, carrying the light of my perception along with it.

And at my behest, this mysterious, playful, flirtatious, yet obedient energy surged upwards like an electric fountain, transforming the sensation of the whole lot into a St Patrick's Day parade of warm, loving tingles.

At first, I didn't know what was happening. I'm still not sure I do. But I knew that the universe was communicating with me by rushing around inside my body. That this thrilling sensation was the true hand of god, if you will. But a god that was also somehow able to obey my directional requests.

I was also kind of wary of the god feeling too, though. Sometimes my whole body would seize up in the grip of her flow, which was instantly fizzing, massaging, inviting, warming. But her presence could be so all-consuming that it felt like being plugged into an electrical socket.

Sometimes it was too much, and I wouldn't know what to do with it all. Eventually, out of necessity, I had to request that she take it a little easier on me; be playful, sure, but a bit less boisterous. And she did.

It was cool reading about her after experiencing her, still with only my own words to describe her.

'Once kundalini is awakened, with consistent practice it can rise up through the central nadi, called Sushumna, that rises up inside or alongside the spine … The progress of kundalini through the different chakras leads to different levels of awakening and mystical experiences.'

thekundaliniyoga.org

I thought how wonderful, how magical, how exciting it was to possess this new dimension of life that felt like Kali sticking her bejewelled thumb up my bum. But what I was yet to learn was that the shakti also has the power to stagnate and even regress.

Later, in 2021, I felt my access to shakti dwindling inside, to quite a concerning degree. Her waters were not as freely flowing, and I could no longer conjure her and instruct her as strongly as I could before.

I worried, 'Am I losing this delicious treat?'

So I hired this fellow off the internet to come round and bathe me in resonant sound. I lay down on my apartment floor with my head on a cushion, and he sat directly behind me like it was a session of psychoanalysis. Out of his big canvas bag of tricks he produced a guitar, some Tibetan singing bowls, and some very science-fiction sounding objects which I couldn't identify because I never laid eyes on them.

However, the overall integrity of the healing became compromised when he began breaking into nineties pop hit covers. Nirvana made a few appearances, as a support act to his big finale which was 4 Non Blondes: 'And I scream from the top of my lungs, *What's going on?*' My thoughts exactly . . .

Wim Hof calls the cold his god. But imagine a religion/cult where all sound, all acoustical vibration was understood as the literal hand/face/voice of god for its ability to remove old skeletons of memory from the body? And fundamentally, we in the cult accept that the 'physical' we are experiencing is really a complex, familiar, partly sonic vibration, and that we are as close to vibrations of sound as we are to form. Who is to say that sound is any less deserving of worship than a bunch of flawed, superhero-style characters from the distant future/past?

After one sound-healing class in Bali – clichés abound – my life felt truly changed. I had let something go that had long wanted out. I thought my feet would never again touch the earth, and was ready to become a full-time devotee to the Church of Sound. I think what happened to me had the opportunity to do so because of the lead-up time spent relaxing the inner focus, which gave the old emotional residue the opportunity to come loose, and then the sound vibration did the rest.

Sound-healing sessions ought to be embraced at a state-sponsored level as a way to keep medical costs down. It is incredibly cheap to administer to large numbers of us, and over time promises huge, core-healing potential.

Not long after the initial waves of euphoria subsided, after the Bali honeymoon, my new lightness of being and vocation to sound began to look a little naive. Because, cosmic irony of ironies, my fame's star ascending to new record heights would be the catalyst to send me crashing back down to Earth.

· Playing Dead ·

I'm in love with all the sounds you make,

Your socks along the floor,

The breaths you have no choice but take.

I'm in my love with what your sounds suggest,

The old, distressed oaken boards,

The space between them tells it best.

If love lies in an invisible place,

Then love has eyes but not a face.

If love calls out in an echoed room,

She's fraudulent and mocks her tomb.

To me love carries more in smell.

Your sweetness is an old bronze bell,

That quiets sounds of needless prayer,

And fills the host with none but air.

The Church of Sound

⌒

Here's a useful inner space technique employing the use of sound.

This is a simple method for getting myself deeply marinating in the rich, creamy sauce of stilasagna. I learned this method from the spiritual teacher Alan Watts.

> 'The easiest way to get into the meditative state is to begin by listening.'
>
> Alan Watts

After some nice, long vagal breaths, and the usual few minutes of fidgeting, once I have collected myself all in one place, I begin listening. Back at the start, I was really *trying* to listen. I'd picked up bad listening habits. It was like that beautiful panoramic mountain view all over again, in that I was kind of pulling and dragging at the sounds I could already hear, as opposed to just hearing them. Thankfully, over time, listening from neutral stillness taught me that *trying* to listen in this way, making any effort to listen, is a pointless! waste of energy. I think I was doing this partly because paying full attention to sound is often referred to as 'active listening'. But really, active listening is something that requires zero activity on my part whatsoever, beyond tuning focus in to the hearing portal of my perception.

This is a particularly useful practice to learn for how to enjoy a good meditation session in really noisy places, like on the train.

With your peepers closed, allow yourself to hear all of the little and large sounds happening around you. As their presence is brought to the attention of awareness, don't identify them, or attach any names to them. Don't explore your opinions about them, or dwell on other times when you've heard them: just hear them. Allow for any and all sounds, echoing in from any and all directions, to pass freely through awareness. So that now your environmental sound becomes like one big 'happening'. One 360-degree halo of sound, happening across one big rippling canvas, like one big sonic hug. In this state, you will notice how no one particular sound coming from one particular direction can be distracting or irritating, even if it's loud or sudden, like the screeching of the train's brakes coming into the station. In this state, you are accepting all sound as one.

Then, you will likely start noticing some of your interior activity – thoughts, sensations, emotions – but treat these 'sounds' in just the same way as you treat the environmental sounds: as something that is happening, and something that you need take no part in.

'What you do is this: as you hear sounds
coming up in your head, thoughts, you
simply listen to them as part of the general
noise going on just as you would be listening

to the sound of my voice or just as you
would be listening to cars going by, or two
birds chattering outside the window. So look
at your own thoughts as just noises. And
soon you will find that the so-called outside
world and the so-called inside world come
together. They are a happening. Your
thoughts are a happening, just like the
sounds going on outside, and everything is
simply a happening and all you're doing is
watching it.'

Alan Watts

When I relate to sound in this way, I begin to deeply embody the
state of pleasurable peaks and ravines of the Volcanoes of Vacantness. Give this practice some time. Don't give up on it early. It
took me a little while to be able to settle in to the hang of this. To
recontextualise the 'sound' of my inner activity as just that. Dwelling on it, the 'noise' initially was uncomfortable, like my mind
was punching me in the face.

Watts goes on to speak about the nature of breathing. How
breathing can be either voluntary or involuntary. Meaning, we can
take conscious breaths, like vagal breathing, but most of the time
when we are focussed on other things, our consciousness takes over
and keeps the breathing mechanism working by itself. But to *watch*
the breath, as it continues breathing in and out by itself, is to demonstrate the fact that the fixed line we draw between 'what we do on
the one hand, and what happens to us on the other, is arbitrary'.

But, for me, just like with the lotus sitting position, this has always been an area of the practice that I have found to be alienating. 'Watching the breath', as a doorway into meditation, is also a central tenet in the Vipassana practice. The Vipassanas are most known these days for running more advanced ten-day-long silent retreats around the world, and watching the breath is central to their practice. But I have never been able to do this, and still can't. As soon as I focus on the aparatus of my breath, it automatically becomes impassive. When my breathing detects the eye of awarenss on it, the gearbox shifts from auto-matic to manual, and my breathing becomes automatically conscious – but without my wanting it to. I want to be able to watch it drift in and out like the tide. I once went on a five-day silent retreat, and the teacher kept referring back to this tech-nique as a direct way in, as a very centring practice, but, in my silence, I was frustrated. Because the more I concentrated on my breath, the less my breath could function smoothly and automatically on its own. It would instead always become me initiating the next breath, instead of the next breath initiating itself. I would mess up the natural rhythm and then, after a while of that, my chest would feel laboured, so I'd give up. I think with this Vipassana technique that they assume that everyone can do this innately, but I'm here to burst that par-ticular bubble (sorry). Perhaps it comes with a little more practice.

Another thing I noticed while employing Watts's technique, listening to both my external sounds and internal sounds as all one happening, was that, scanning downwards, how easy it becomes to wilfully forget all of the names (stories) that would typically be attached to the sensations of my being: my body, my hands, face, legs, eyes, teeth, etc.

I came to see that the physical aspect of my being, and the labels that I had assigned to it, were completely separate and different things.

Dropping all the identifications was to discover my existence for what it really is: a weight of perception in the darkness. A concentrated murmuration of acoustic, magnetic and holographic energy, all rippling across a three-dimensional field.

Identifications are useful in the big, bad material world, but in here, they are of no use. See if you can drop the labels like they're hot, to further enrich a nice, emptying bowl of beingness. Because beingness truly begins when one stops identifying (with) things.

Moving deeply into that field is what this book is all about. It might not feel like much at first; it might feel pointless! It might even feel palpably uncomfortable, but that is only because it's the first step in a lifelong adventure. Everyone feels a bit achey and sore after the first day's hike, it's only natural. The bodymind, particularly its mental activity (talking head), needs time to adapt to this new inward course you are setting for it. Its whole life it has striven to be dynamic in movement and dynamic in thought. But now, it is kindly being asked to put movement to one side altogether and embrace movement's opposite: stillness.

Moving into that field gives one's whole physical aspect the opportunity to be seen anew, and seen directly, as opposed to being understood symbolically. And it brings us closer to the source of all the good ideas that there have ever been.

Why not try taking a gentle moment here, closing your eyes, and seeing how much of your physical body you can perceive without naming any of it?

At first, it may only be for the amount of time it takes to go to the toilet in the morning. Or to sink deeply into the soles of your feet and listen to the flowing water in the shower. Or to stand on the street with your eyes closed and listen to all of the sounds of the city, like one would listen to Beethoven's 'Ode to Joy'.

Later on, you will want to do this for longer time, that is the beauty of it: every second spent in space is its own reward. No amount of time is wasted time.

And if it feels a little awkward at first, and you end up saying 'fuck it' the first few times, well, welcome to the club.

Fame!

I wanna live ... Well, not forever, but long enough

Once, in Taupō, on the North Island of New Zealand, I snatched a phone out of a girl's hand and frisbeed it full-force across the smoking area of a bar. I had the weekend off from filming, so I'd hit the mountain-biking trails of Tongariro National Park. An Irish fellow from the hostel called Micheál and I were drinking in the last bar open, which contained quite a few members of the NZ branch of the Bloods. They wore fashionable matching red sport coats with the group's insignia embossed on the back, and red bandanas tied across the bridges of their noses to hide their faces. Anyway, this girl wandered up grinning from ear to ear with her phone held in front of her like she was already filming. What happened then came as a surprise to us both as we watched her phone go sailing over the heads of the Bloods. Next thing, her right hook descends, but I parry it with just enough spirit to prevent the full land. Roars of excitement and confusion squirrel up from the crowd. Then, next to come flying were the contents of her gin-and-tonic. Splash! All over my face. It was March-ish time though, and Taupō was humid as fuck, so the dowse actually came as an unexpectedly pleasant surprise. A bouncer with whom we'd had a nice chat on the way in appeared at my side looking baffled. He put his hand on my shoulder and turned me around quick and ushered us out of the emergency exit. Micheál and I speed-walked home, speechless . . .

I struggled with the sudden change of circumstances known as fame. I'm a strange enough bird anyway, and as fame grew, I could feel it greying my feathers.

Real, proper fame arrived early 2019-ish. I'd been a bit famous before that, but after the release of *The Umbrella Academy* on planet TV, that was when the real, proper fame arrived. Nobody could have prepared me for the swiftness of the dissolution and renegotiation of the social contract between me and the rest of humanity.

Netflix distribution is so vast and immediate, the marketing so well-funded in reach, that it was like being injected in the arse cheek with a giant fame-booster. It's easier to list the countries in the world where Netflix is currently not available.

China, Crimea, North Korea, Russia and Syria.

Reed Hastings, co-creator of Netflix, called it 'the birth of a global TV network'.

After our show's glorious success, it was the realisation of a long-harboured dream. Here I was getting to act a delightfully weird part on a wonderfully written, unique show, playing a character who is beloved on a global scale. In this day and age, if you're asking for more than that as an actor, then you're a very greedy boy.

After it came out, life changed jarringly swiftly. At first, my feeling was that most of this change – in fact all of this change – happened in you, the rest of the world, not me. But then again, at the same time, I'd also been changing loads over the previous couple of years. Through the practice I was becoming more settled. Having earned more space inside to allow for creativity, contemplation and self-awareness (the good kind), I was excitedly bringing that transformation into work to explore playing somebody who lacks a great deal of self-awareness.

As I was evolving how I relate to my own emotions, I had the pleasure of playing someone who cannot control his. Someone who knows deep down what pain barriers he must cross to feel less pain, but refuses to cross them because it's too painful. I believe my success, when it came to Klaus specifically, is as a direct result of the stuff I was going through in practising meditation. Learning the art of becoming still. My acting career owes the practice a great deal.

Truman Capote did once say to me at a cocktail party, 'More tears are shed over answered prayers than unanswered ones.' I wouldn't quite go that far; the only tears I shed for our success were psychic tears of joy, I can tell you. But as I was expanding beyond the boundary of old painful emotions, simultaneously I was becoming famous for playing someone who is a complete emotional wreck.

And as these two opposing forces grew, all entangled together in one life, *fame!* became difficult for me.

I felt as though something of the true connection between humanity and me became breached. A little wear and tear in the wiring, perhaps. 'Perhaps I should call an electrician, but if I do and he recognises me, will he overcharge?'

After transmission of *The Umbrella Academy* it went from being, 'Oh, look, it's that guy from *Misfits*. Should we get a photo?' To, 'Oh my god, it's that guy from planet TV – we *have* to get a photo. This could be our only chance.'

Your face popping up on other people's brightly lit search-engine screens at other tables in the cafe/restaurant/bar/everywhere, but not before the rubberneck move: the wide-eyed look, then the hush and huddle over the smartphone. Then the clandestine group vote to see who's going to go over there and ask whether or not it's him and can we have a photo.

Your neck being grabbed hold of by overly sugared, drunken louts who have confused volume with charm again, as they try to 'pal' and 'buddy' you into surrendering to whatever whim they're currently possessed by.

Them: Hey! You're not that guy, are you?
Me: No.
Them: You *are* that guy! Oh my god.
Me: Yes.
Them (*eyes narrow*): Nah, you're *not* that guy.

Folks abandoning their initially chosen route to cross the road and follow you instead, and then quantum-leaping from starry-eyed to spiteful in about 0.6 seconds when you don't want to take the photo. People jumping out of cars in the middle of traffic brandishing smartphones. People photographing and filming you on buses and trains and at airports, while doing a terrible job at trying to make it look like they're not filming you.

A woman started photographing me recently as I was shoving my suitcase up into the upper storage compartment on an airplane. In that bit! That cramped and awkward bit of travel where everyone just wants to sit down and retreat into their own little bubbles.

Getting both barrels of the Diana treatment by paparazzi as

you walk down a busy shopping street with your mother. And you can see, through the flashes, that your mother doesn't know whether it's best to flee or to stand by her son. And you feel a sudden surge of gratitude for the fact that you're wearing sunglasses, since you've been up the whole night before taking ecstasy.

Or being cornered in a downstairs pub corridor by a bunch of tough-looking shouty lads, eyes all bulging out of their heads as they produce two eight-balls worth of cocaine that could have us all put away for ten years and request, friendlily at first, that you do some with them. When you decline as respectfully as possible, a particularly beefy one in a navy tracksuit steps right up into your face: 'You're fake, you are. These lads might not be able to see it, but I can see right through you.'

You finish your pint quickly and go somewhere else. Slinking out the front door with your eyes down, like you're the defendant in a murder trial who's just been taken out of the back of the prison van.

Now, I must pause here and assert that I'm only listing all these negative experiences upfront to make the point that in the early days, my opinion of this new found mega-fame was not a very positive one. But I am grateful that now, that has changed.

Early on, even with all the nice things happening – like the kind words and admiration and respect, the reverence bestowed upon me from the racing hearts of people proclaiming that my work had given them great meaning in their lives – it was still somehow all amounting to a feeling of less connection to other people, not more. Like I'd been put inside a double-glazed glass display cabinet. More invisible, ironically, not less. And it got to a place where if someone did approach me after recognising me off the TV, passively I began to disregard them as a real human being. Exchanging niceties, being courteous and the minimum of charming, but truthfully I dismissed them and disavowed them of all their human complexity by relegating them to the 'fan zone'.

It was like how I always thought it must feel to win the lottery. Sure, now you have all the money in the world at your disposal, but what good is it when none of your friends and family ever speak to you the same way ever again?

There came a point, about a year or two after landing on planet *fame!*, that if I'd had the opportunity to rub a golden lamp, or maybe a nice aquamarine ceramic lamp painted in the style of 1750s Japanese erotica, I'd have wished to go back three times over.

Anxiety grew. Not to stay too long among large crowds of other human doings. A nagging worry that my fame was casting a shadow over not just my own night, but my friends' and families' nights too. A flinch, if a loud bozo approached straightaway looking for something off me – a pic, a lock, a sock, a cock, a vial of blood.

A departure of ease which, after a few drinks, had the potential to express itself unhelpfully, like, 'You want a what? A picture? I've none on me I'm afraid but I do have these shoes and about eight quid in change. What size are you?'

And an emptiness, at night's end, after having disentangled ourselves from the fevered throng thinking, 'I tried to join in, I really did . . .'

Fame! She's a tricky customer. It even distorted familiar dynamics within my own family and friends, through no one's fault. When I got famous enough that it seemed like everyone in

Ireland was treating me like the mayor, awarding me a certain seniority, this was brand-new territory for everyone to navigate.

More and more, if some random ran up without even so much as a hello or a handjob, asking for a photograph or whatever, it was making me feel worthless.

At the same time, attempts to claw back some steady ground under my feet meant kind of leaning into the *fame!* Or letting the *fame!* lead, if you will, which, in that unsteady emotional state, only upped risks of getting more fully on board with the strangely debasing role of it all. This was the stuff of the mask that began eating hungrily into my face.

If that happens, you're fucked. I've met a few famous people who somewhere along the road allowed themselves to get overly inflated by all the praise afforded them, and as such, their energy is off. By late 2019-ish, meeting a person who had no prior knowledge of me felt like a novel relief.

An opportunity on which to pounce like a randy porcupine. I am not suggesting for a moment that porcupine sex is anything but consensual, frankly I wouldn't know. I was once in a zoo. And there was a huge, badass porcupine with a quiff striking a pose like Danny Zucco. And as I leaned over the concerningly low wall, he began marching, slowly and ominously, towards me, bristling up his back needles. But then, he stopped dead only three feet away, and we held each other's gazes for what felt like ages. Both of us, slowly tickling the air around our sidearms. Then, as the sun rolled out from the hill behind me and glared directly into his eyes, I took my chance and backed off.

The sudden quantum *fame!* leap was scary at first – not because I was suffering from becoming overly inflated, but because I was suffering from it in the opposing direction. *Fame!* was deflating me like a wrinkled balloon. I was suffering because, after a few encounters with people whose energies I was not yet equipped to deal with, I developed an instinctive resistance to it. I reverted to auto-resistance mode. I was unable to resign myself to the mild panic about how, from now on, it was going to be way harder to forge real and worthwhile connections with the rest of all of you. That idea broke my heart because, like my father Joe, I get a lot of my energy from connecting with other people. Without being fully aware of it, I began to resist the change that *fame!* was bringing about. I suffered because I wrongly identified this new road of *fame!*, and the manifestation of it in others, from which there was no return, as a dead end. A dangerous thing, a ruinous thing. A quiet despair, like it was too late to recoup what I'd lost. 'Famous Rob' was wondering how to stuff the genie back into the bottle, all the while thinking, 'Hang on a second, when we last met weren't you living in an erotic Japanese lamp?'

And confirmation biases are subtle, wouldn't you agree? They sneak up on you. A confirmation bias is defined thus:

> *Confirmation bias (noun): The tendency to seek or favour new information which supports one's existing theories or beliefs, while avoiding or rejecting that which disrupts them.*
> – Oxford English Dictionary

When something happens, a confirmation bias arrives in your awareness (or not at all) like a small satisfactory 'click'. An 'Oh yeah, I know what's happening here.' It can be a pleasing click, because it assures us that we kind of know before we know, you know? But we often don't.

They are often imperceptible, meaning the ability to detect one's own confirmation bias as a response to whatever situation is not consciously present, and once they remain unnoticed long enough they become part of the wallpaper. Confirmation biases are like typical movie scripts in that they've got a three-act structure.

☆ **Act one:** identifying an event that is happening in your external world by back-referencing a past experience.

☆ **Act two:** the meaning of that event is then falsely deduced or 'confirmed'.

☆ **Act three:** the event is stored as yet more evidence to confirm the bias that possesses its host, and then it grows even more tendrils of protoplasm like a slime mould.

'Uncertainty is an uncomfortable position.
But certainty is an absurd one.'

Voltaire

Confirmation biases are self-imposed prisons. And, after *fame!* ramped up several degrees, I began (re)confirming my *fame!* in the behaviour of others as a source of danger. Helped on by the growing numbers of scandalous stories of some unsavoury famous people, *fame!* incrementally morphed into something that needed to be watched out for. Heat-sought in the body jerks and twitches of other members of the public in my locale.

I've also seen the wreckage of this in other famous people. A wariness and a weariness in public. Which enforces my own prejudice that, just in the same way that getting better at doing nothing gives you a larger sense of everything, *fame!* condemns the famous the same way as it exalts. I would wager a shiny shilling that an unhoused person, a person begging on the streets of London, feels the exact same feelings of alienation and invisibility in their bodies as one of the members of his royal family.

For a while, I definitely used too much weed and alcohol to run away from coping with the new terms and conditions.

I once used to describe my before-sleep overthinking to others as, 'God, sometimes when my head hits the pillow at night, it lights up like a fuckin' firecracker.' Which serves as a good reminder of how I always had a habit of hiding from myself through the language of euphemism. I euphemised the language that caused me emotional discomfort to directly name out loud. 'Booze', there's a good one.

Popping onto the internet for the craic, the first website I scroll down for 'alcohol slang terms' yields 148 different euphemisms. Such as 'giggle water', 'moonshine', 'nectar of the gods', 'liquid courage' and, ah, 'nightcap, anyone?'

Quentin Crisp once said this to me while we were fishing in the Amazon, 'Euphemisms are unpleasant truths wearing diplomatic cologne.'

They not only have the power to soften the emotional blow but also to add an aire of glamour. Ones like 'Out boozin'' or 'On the jar for three days straight!' once inspired in me a kind of heady, decadent coolness. It possessed an aroma of enchantment to a young person who was seeking to transform.

I have another friend who enjoys drinking alcohol. And when it's late he'll shake the bottle, shrug and say, 'nasty lasty'? Which is just a top class alternative euphemism for 'nightcap'. For when you're all drinking and it's late, and you all want another one but you know you probably shouldn't. Until one drinker shines a beam of possibility over the guilt barrier that you're all hoping to pass over together, for that is the only way across.

This is by no means meant to come across as a condemnation of drinking. I'm very much on the side of drinking.

Alcohol is often euphemised according to its volumetric measure. A half. A single. A double. A shot. A pint. Oh, just seeing the word 'pint' written down conjures up an image. Of a freshly poured fizzy, foggy beer, all frothing over the top of the glass. And all around it are my friends, chatting and bursting into sporadic laughter in the fullness of their voices. And the pub all around the 'pint' is lively. There's a bustling wedge of other punters all doing the same thing: communing together as one big throng. And we're right in the middle of an animated, meaningful, trusting, undistracted chat. A 'pint' casts a powerful spell. It inspires my salivary glands to go. It conjures in me a strong sensation of social cohesion, and invokes a cask-worth of connections gone by. For a long time, if I'm honest, as long as I felt I had shown enough restraint, and been productive enough to feel like it was earned, having a pint was when I felt the most happy. That or having sex. And back then love was still something that was attached to sex, not the other way around. The 'pint' was a joy outmatched only by the heights of intermittent moments performing on stage, where one could be liable to experience religious levels of loss of self – but those moments were much rarer. Back then, my relationship to happiness and its pursuit could've been visually represented by steep, jagged spikes going across a graph, like a lie detector.

After arriving on planet *fame!*, alcohol and weed were the substances that gave me back a social appetite. I used them as crutches. No hiding behind euphemisms here, *fame!* brought with her some addiction issues.

In ways, weed and alcohol wound back the clock. For a while anyway, they provided a route back to a more mischievous and carefree Rob. Until they began to make me more egotistical, flaky and unable to focus on what anyone was saying for very long.

But instead of reducing and stopping, as you would, I persisted. Even though smoking too much was creating unwanted side-effects, like occasional dizzy spells, unreasonable sweating and forgetfulness, I continued to medicate *fame!* as my own little 'social disability'.

I was scared to look directly at it because of what it might mean to look.

In the background, this was only serving to drag me right back to square one. To lower my self-esteem and turn me into a coward – and still I kept refusing to examine what was really going on. It was like being right back there in Portland, hiding from myself once again. Keeping the door firmly wedged shut on a life that had a clear will of its own to change in a different direction.

The (false) *fame!* story that I was telling myself and had convinced myself of was: 'I am more fun and interesting when I am high.' Therefore, by definition according to the *Tao Te Ching*, in the shadow the opposite was also true: 'I am *less* fun and *less* interesting to be around sober.' There was enough going on in me to warrant requiring a kind of sedation, to avoid having to bump up against an inferior version of myself in the presence of other people.

I craved my night-time 'edge', like Dr Jekyll. Sure, Jekyll knew there were problems involved with being Hyde, but he still couldn't resist unlocking that cage. He became obsessed with the animal freedoms and loss of stifling self-inhibition he was denied but which Hyde could afford.

He drank down his green potion and his face came off like a mask, and all the burdensome weight fell off with it. That old chestnut. I even remember thinking, 'If I spend enough time as Hyde, then I'll forget all about being Jekyll and not need weed anymore, right?' Oh, the ribbons of bullshit.

· Playing Dead ·

Fretful night,

Dreaded craving,

Screen light

Licks the cracks of the street paving.

Heavy head,

Fifty pound,

Drops what it's carrying

All over the ground.

What prevents me

From staying still?

Decrying the effect

Of a sleeping pill.

What weight of waking load is borne,

Where sleep collapses into form?

I'd no crave 'til the crave was put

Inside the labyrinthine wall of gut.

In the rankled phlegm of metallic paint

Streaks snarls of flashing self-restraint,

All daubed in pink italic font:

When the fuck do I get what I want?

Again, I must stress that I paint an overly negative and one-sided picture of *fame!* here because that was the story that took centre stage early on.

But, luckily for me, the universe has a habit of dropping breadcrumbs. Around late summer of 2019, about half a year into being stranded on planet *fame!*, I was living in a semi-dilapidated former shoe factory in Toronto on the corner of Queen and Ontario, while making season two of *The Umbrella Academy*. The former shoe factory has since been bulldozed amidst the brutal onslaught of property development, and turned into yet another architecturally featureless cookie-cutter condo building. One evening, while carrying home the shopping, I noticed a shifty-looking man in a beanie sitting on the front stoop having a smoke.

So I challenged him to a game of 'who can urinate the highest on the adjoining alleyway wall'. If I won, then he had to give me the contents of his wallet and never come back to the stoop ever again. And if he won, I had to sing the entire Greek national anthem in a nearby local necropolis. Not only did he win but he cleared the alleyway wall entirely, and sprinkled the roof of a discontinued soft-top convertible Pontiac Solstice that was parked on the other side. Luckily for me he was merciful and did not insist on the forfeit, so the Greek dead got to rest in their crypts untroubled.

Later, after we got him out on bail, we became pals. In my unit on the fifth floor, I had a beautiful old antique chess set, and many evenings Dinesh would come round and school me. We'd smoke and chat into the small hours, mostly about creative ideas on how to fix the climate problem. And one night, I was grumbling away mindlessly on the subject of my *fame!*: 'The weirdness of it all is making me wonder if it wouldn't be best just to quit acting altogether. Put my energy somewhere where it would be better put to use. Draw a line under it all and start afresh. But then, does that really change anything? I mean, it's not as if my *fame!* would suddenly vanish in a poof of smoke if I did . . .'

That's when the universe offered a breadcrumb, when he said: 'Why not try just accepting it all, man? The new story of your fame. I mean, it's here, it's not going away. You have little choice. Have you tried that strategy?'

Have you ever had that experience where you read something, or someone says something to you, and straightaway you know that it's the course of action you must take? Even though you have no idea how to do it yet. Like a light switching on inside. As soon as Dinesh said that, I knew he was right. And the realisation dawned that it was not being stranded on planet *fame!* that was causing my struggle, but my resistance to it. Even though I'd worked my entire life towards getting there. It was not *fame!* itself but my own confirmation bias that *fame!* was a nuisance and a danger. It was my inability to accept this new change. That was the real stuff of the mask that was eating into my face.

At the core of the teachings of Buddhism, there is something called 'the Four Noble Truths'. They are the essence of Buddha's teachings.

Over 2,500 years ago, he was quoted as saying: 'I teach suffering, its origin, cessation and path. That is all I teach.' Buddha was a very practical psychologist.

The four noble truths are as follows:

1. **The truth of suffering, or *dukkha*.**
   Dukkha means the inevitability that there is suffering. And as we go through life we *inevitably* suffer at times. *Dukkha*

doesn't just mean 'to suffer'; it can also be translated as 'temporary' or 'inevitable', or 'conditional', even 'precious'. It can take the form of sickness, old age or imminent death. And even when we are not suffering from any of these, suffering comes in plenty of other forms.

2. **The truth of the cause of suffering, or *samudāya*.**
Buddha reasoned like a physician. He rightly concluded that if there is suffering going on, then the first step to healing it is finding its cause. But he went one step further and claimed that all suffering has just one cause. And that is, very simply put, attachment. Attachment arrives in the forms of craving or (misplaced) desire, ignorance or delusion, anger or hatred. I want to make it clear I do not include bodily suffering here, like chronic pain or diseases, the cause of which sometimes the sufferer can do nothing about.

3. **The truth of the way out of suffering, or *nirodha*.**
Once the cause of suffering has been discovered, the next step is to believe that there is a cure. Buddha taught that the way to liberate oneself from the cause of suffering – be it the desire to possess more money, or possess somebody, or hurt somebody, etc. – is to practise the art of non-attachment. Non-attachment means the ability to experience what is there to be perceived through the senses, one's subjective reality, without becoming enchanted or misled by it into suffering. Feeling the strong will of desire well up inside, but instead of surrendering to it and being blindly compelled by it, non-attachment is to simply be present with it.

4. **The truth of the path out of suffering, or *magga*.**
   This was Buddha's prognosis. Having identified that the
   common denominator that unites all suffering is attachment,
   or, in other words, the inability to not be at the total surrender
   of one's own desires or aversions, his solution to this is
   something known as 'the middle way'. Because it is a path
   that avoids too much indulgence on one side, and too much
   severe asceticism on the other. Neither of which Buddha
   found helpful to him on his path to becoming enlightened.

To *accept* fame, eh? To embrace this new, unpredictable and
seemingly inhospitable landscape of planet *fame!*? Even the
notion of this idea, at first, felt internally difficult. It bumped up
against something very solid inside me, something that felt physical. Like a wall.

But newly inspired, after Dinesh left I nestled deeply into the
couch for a nice long, delicious mindfulness session, to fully
unroll my whole *fame!* story scroll.

Relaxing into the depths of being meant being better
equipped to take a cooler, calmer, more sober view of it all in
greater detail. All of the memories, sensations and beliefs that naturally wanted to froth up to the surface. I scanned the *fame!* story's
contents, as much as I could perceive of it, for hidden porcupine
needles of negativity. I kept a keen third eye open for stories
coming up whose themes generally reflected negativity/unpleas-
antness/shock/discomfort, etc., and found the whole thing rife.
My *fame!* story, which I'd inadvertently been (re)telling and re-
enforcing both to myself and out loud, had become a pageant
parade made up of shoddily constructed papier-maché floats connected by spiteful, rhythmless marching bands.

Unsurprisingly, the first things to come hurtling up of their own accord were the unsavoury incidents. Like the times I'd quietly hated myself for capitulating and going along with whatever requests for the purposes of not upsetting strangers. Or the times *fame!* had freaked me out, like a woman screaming 'Fuck you! Fuck you!' while pursuing me down the street after I refused to pose for a photo.

But then, as a result of my polite yet persistent requests of my own unconscious, other memories that had received far less airtime eventually began to emerge. Starting with the more transient ones, like the many cool people I'd gotten to meet over the years, and the interesting places I'd gotten to travel to, and in relative luxury.

One choice example was travelling to a tiny town in Western Australia called Pinjarra, to act in a movie called *Three Summers*. It was written and directed by Ben Elton, of whom I once enquired, 'Ben, do you mind me going off script every now and again and improvising a little when it feels right?' 'Oh, not at all, Rob,' he replied, 'Go right ahead. But I'll tell you now, I'll give you cash, no credit.'

For the film's folk-music festival campground setting, the same festival that takes place over three summers, we were shooting on indigenous land. It was a magical place vibrating with life. Kangaroos abounded, hopping all over the shop. Once, we stalked a kangaroo through thickets of bush on a golf cart, and he kept stopping every fifty or so yards just so we could catch up with him. Or at least that's what we told ourselves.

And there were these big green, black and yellow cockatoos everywhere, known as twenty-eights, who had the softest, most enchanting call. They sat high up in the trees but would also roam around pecking away at the ground.

On the eve of filming's commencement, we all gathered together to take part in a Welcome to Country ritual.

We'd spent that whole afternoon learning about our new pals and fellow cast, the Bindjareb Nyungar people, by hiking into sacred land and collecting dry grass and kangaroo poop; all the necessary ingredients we would need for the ritual's ceremonial fire. Then, as early evening fell, and the sun oranged behind the trees, the Nyungar elder, Kuda, kicked off proceedings by speaking directly to his ancestors, who he could sense watching us from all around. When he said he could see the spirits of the Stolen Generations sitting watching us from above in the trees, it sent chills down my spine. Kuda thanked them warmly for having the grace to allow a film crew to come in and galumph all over the place. And then he invited all the men forward to form a line to get the fire going the old-fashioned way, using pure friction. As man after man after man heaved his full weight down on that hand drill, swivelling with all his might in hopes to be the one to court the smoking kindling into that first lick of flame, all the women stood around in a circle cat-calling us for not making the fire happen faster.

'Come on, you wimps! Chop-chop, we're chilly already!' Et cetera.

And then, after *twenty-two minutes*, as I remember, of group swivelling and sweating, we the mighty men finally made fire. Well, we leapt and frolicked around in shared triumph, like we'd just performed a miracle. Like we were the first ever humans to make fire. It was brilliant. Alchemising fire out of sheer collective back-breaking labour gave us such an enormous uplift of happiness as a group that that was it: we were bonded together for the rest of the shoot. These are the experiences to be commemorated and savoured, not forgotten under the bad ones.

And, as I settled deeper still into my old *fame!* story search, I began to relive times that made me immensely proud and gave me untold joy.

Like on our big opening night of the Shakespearean trilogy *The Wars of the Roses*, in which I played the villainous hump-backed King Richard III. 'Opening night' refers to the night that the newspaper critics are finally let in to watch, so nerves and excitement are at fever pitch. Afterwards, still coursing with adrenaline, I came downstairs into the theatre bar to see everyone buzzing, and was met by my friend and acting father Michael Ironside, with tears rolling down his face as he proclaimed, 'You tore the shit off the walls!' He was right, too. And on that same night, the show's PR man, who had promoted both Laurence Olivier's and my Richard III, told me how he thought my performance was better.

Playing Richard was an enormous, terrifying challenge and as such, is up there as one of the most thrilling and rewarding parts I've ever got to play.

The *fame!* story continued to take me back and back. All the way back to looking at my relationship with *fame!*, long before landing on its planet. Back to the times when I thirsted for it. Like when I was nineteen years old and had just done a bit part on an ensemble TV thing called *Rock Rivals*. And when it aired, I went out in Dublin the next day and made sure to hang around in crowded places with my brother, Brendan, just to see if anyone would recognise me.

Lastly, there has been no stage or camera appearance that has given me more satisfaction and pride than the times I have held the clammy hands of a complete stranger, their voices excited and wobbly as they tell me that they, or their close loved one, found genuine laughter and levity through one of my performances in the middle of hard times. That my work was able to give another real person real joy. Now that's the stuff that deserves to be the headline of the *fame!* story. That I, in my own peculiar way, on this little blue planet of ours, have had the pleasure of alleviating another person's suffering. If I could bottle that misty feeling, I'd be a billionaire.

Then, as a bit of Nils Frahm droned and pinged atmospherically in the background, suddenly I could see the truth. That my whole *fame!* story's theme really had a hugely positive aggregate, and I'd been telling myself a negatively slanted, narrowed and false version of it.

Just by stepping back from the activity of my individual, through embracing the feeling of velvet-y vacantness, I was given eyes to more clearly discern what confirmation bias I'd been carrying around, irrespective of whatever external things were happening.

Then, I found myself for the first time in a position to ask the question: 'Am I really going to allow this narrowed version of my *fame!*, the version where it's painful and dangerous and unwelcome, to create unpleasantness and resistance in me for the rest of my life? Every time I'm out, and someone whose behaviour I can't control behaves in a way that I don't like because it is similar to the way someone has acted before, is that really going to be enough to throw a spanner in my works?'

I thought: 'But what does it matter really what the past is, over and above how it's making me presently feel? Can I *really* accept fame? Is it even possible to wholeheartedly welcome something that has caused me such misery? Could I at least experiment by reframing all of this fame stuff as a gift? Taking it as a given that I will probably act more in my life (because let's be honest, I'm fabulous at it), what is the point in standing so loyally by such an unhelpful version of things? And maybe – who knows until I try – being closer to the fringes of the human herd could be as valid and interesting a place to create from, if not more so, as nearer the centre? Dare I to dream . . . ? But would it be aiming way too high to try to get to a place where fame becomes a part of my life I can actually tailor-make and *enjoy*? Only fools refuse good advice when it's given, and one can find great freedom in restraint, so why not try embracing these ropes with which I feel tied first *before* trying to wriggle out of them?'

And the answer to all these questions was: '*Fame!* I want you to live . . . Well, not forever, but long enough.'

From out of this burgeoning, fledgling seed of acceptance – wouldn't you know it? – a natural compassion around the discomfort of *fame!* began to grow.

It began to engulf my automatic discomfort. So that my tailoring of *fame!* became more about making sure that I was taking care of what I needed before taking care of other people's needs. From the perspective of self-compassion, it became possible to trial new ways of refusing requests when I felt like it, but while still offering love.

I tested little techniques to manage people's expectations and help snap them more quickly out of the TV spell.

Here is an example of one such technique:

Them: Hey, could I get a photo?
Me: No.

But over time, the 'no' became a more refined 'no'. A practised 'no'. A 'no' like wine from an old Italian vintners. A 'no' that has had time to marinate, just like the mantra. That had been given a chance to mature and grow, to the point of carrying no superfluous emotions on its back.

Most importantly, the 'no' had to mature to the point of side-stepping any primal fizzes of confrontation so that we could both get on with our days unrocked. Because no (wo)man is an island; we are all emotional satellites vibrating off one another, and what is said between two strangers is secondary to what's felt.

Another useful skill that came out of embracing Dinesh's acceptance strategy was learning how to swiftly and effectively let go of another person's frantic, unwanted energy that had found its way inside my body.

Be it faming, flirting, foraging, doing of any kind, this advice still applies well:

'Be like water making its way through cracks … If nothing within you stays rigid, outward things will disclose themselves. Empty your mind, be formless. Shapeless, like water. If you put water into a cup, it becomes the cup. You put water into a bottle and it becomes the bottle. You put it in a teapot, it becomes the teapot … Be water, my friend.'

Bruce Lee

Bruce knew the score. Strength is not in how hard we punch, but how well we can roll with the punches. I'd have still kicked his ass, though.

So now, I can truthfully declare that this book owes its very creation to my sudden and quite jarring explosion of *fame!*, but only after its seed was finally watered and allowed to grow. And for that, it follows that I hold legitimate cause to be grateful to those feelings of misery and alienation granted to me by landing on this strange new planet.

My perceived *samudāya* was the sudden change in life brought about by the success of *The Umbrella Academy*. It was not *fame!*, but my aversion to the story of *fame!* that grew inside my head. And led me to cling helplessly on to the past and resist the present. Which led to a closedness, which led in turn to me disliking myself more and more. Particularly in the company of people who recognised me, even if they were complimenting me about my work. I mean, isn't that mad? In how many other professions does somebody get to have that? Strangers walking up to them on the street and complimenting them about their work? But for me, even this was soured. Because you lovely, kind-hearted people were being confirmed as the embodiment of the thing that I least liked about myself.

It was easier just to blame *fame!*, blame all of this 'stifling recognition'. When really, it was you recognisers who symbolised *my own* inability to enjoy my life. To be changeful and go with the natural flow of the present. Which is the only real choice we have, and if we make a different one, the result is suffering.

My *nirodha* was my friend Dinesh. Because he was the one who showed me that there was another way to go about it. My *magga* was to observe, re-evaluate, and ultimately re-edit this *fame!* story that I'd been (re)enforcing to myself and out loud to other people. And my *magga* was also practising being present enough to notice my *fame!* confirmation bias whenever it reared its head. Being present enough to feel how I am feeling, so as to remain unattached from my feelings, having discerned that surrendering to and becoming enchanted by such feelings only leads to suffering.

Here is a really simple and effective exercise to try. It's typically done first thing in the morning, but it can be done any time of the day or night.

I don't know about you but once I wake up, my head wants to be three steps ahead of my body. Checking my phone, rushing downstairs and getting on with the jobs that need doing. I've always been a sleeper-in too, so once I'm finally up and about, I find myself galloping ahead to try to claw back lost time. Traditionally, this has led to a frantic morning head and negatively affects my mood.

There is a Buddhist practice, sometimes called the *lokah samastah* mantra. *Lokah* is a Sanskrit word roughly meaning 'realm' or 'world', and *samastah* refers to all of the beings in the world.

Taking a second just after waking to sit upright and collect yourself, and check in with what you're feeling through a nice bodyscan. And then silently say:

Today,

May I be happy.

May I be healthy.

May life be free from pain and suffering,

May life be full of joy and ease.

Try saying it three times slowly to yourself, all the while noticing any little emotional objections to those invitations that pop up. Any feelings that bump up against the meaning of these words:

May I allow for the possibility of being happy,

May I be strong, and healthy as a racehorse who has just

walked the Grand National,

May all pain and suffering pearl off me like water off a

duck's back,

And may life be brimming over with love, laughter, ease,

craic, mischief and connection to other ducks just like me.

And then, the affirmation for the rest of the beings of the world:

May *you* be happy.

May you be healthy.

May your life be free of all pain and suffering.

And be chock-full of joyfulness and ease.

Giving yourself and others this invitation only takes a second but its effects are long. It sets you up with a strong emotional template that ripples throughout the day. What else do you need? Oh yeah, breakfast.

A younger man was rearranged

To hear a piece of art he changed

Into a ridgebacked dinosaur,

Who lived ten feet under the floor.

Ground to halt the gramophone,

Bade ridgeback skull and porous bone

Leap skilfully up through the cracks

Of carefully laden floorboard tracks.

A man once more though still quite young,

His quest refused to grace his tongue,

Which panted dryly in his skull,

Where emptiness was plentiful.

Une Dérive

I am fascinated by psychogeography. Psychogeography is the study of a place's character, and the impact that that character has on how we feel and behave while we are there.

Why do some environments in town invite certain types of behaviour and not others? Psychogeography looks at the 'soul' of a place, which is intuited through its atmosphere and expressed bodily through us. As a school of thought, psychogeography covers a lot of different ground (pun intended).

The aspect of it I'm most interested in is the idea that a place, like for example the Liberties in Dublin city, beyond just its bricks and mortar is first and foremost a story. A story that is directly responsible for giving rise to its character.

A good psychogeographical example is St Giles Square, an area situated in the West End of London. It sits at the junction where Charing Cross Road and New Oxford Street converge. Despite London's attempts to give it a makeover by lacquering shiny buildings over the top of it, the old rot somehow still rises up to dampen the pavements. Going back further, from the Middle Ages and up to the fifteenth century, the junction was the site of a public gallows, complete with a cage to display the prisoners so they could be afforded generous helpings of public shame. Later, in 1761, a bricklayer called John Duke was buried there for murdering his wife and then himself. A wooden stake was driven through him 'to earth-fasten the body', whereby the ghost is shackled to the spot and robbed of its natural passing. Unknowingly, still to this day, London roars over his memory. Right up to the nineteenth century, that area was a slum or a 'rookery', notorious for criminality and debauchery. The St Giles rookery, wryly known as 'the Holy Land', was a slum made infamous as the face of the gin epidemic in William Hogarth's mid-eighteenth century painting *Gin Lane*.

The Liberties in Dublin City is an old pocket in the central south-west of Dublin. Back in the twelfth century, it first emerged as a settlement outside of the walled city of Átha Cliath (The Crossing of the Hurdles/Dublin). And at that time, Dublin's judicial system, security and trade were all controlled by a corporation that levied the taxes. But the 'Liberty' signified the area beyond the corporation's control.

The Liberty settlement was part of a large swathe of lands to the west of the city given by King Henry II to the Augustinian monks to establish the Abbey of St Thomas the Martyr. They owned the Liberties until the mid-sixteenth century, until Henry VIII started dissolving all the monasteries in the Reformation. At which point, ownership passed solely into the hands of a one William Brabazon.

Brabazon was a patron, trusted ally and political puppet of Thomas Cromwell. He was made vice treasurer in 1534, a role that meant he had full control of all the British money flowing into Ireland.

Despite his role as a glorified financial administrator, he was fiercely colonially minded, and actually distinguished himself by leading clashes against the Irish Gaels attempting to reclaim their stolen lands, like the FitzGeralds in 1535 led by the famous Silken Thomas. The FitzGeralds had watched as Henry's VIII's forces enacted the dissolution of all the monasteries and therefore town-lands in their home of the province of Leinster, and along with that, vast areas were forcefully jettisoned, garrisoned and replanted as British. Shortly after this, Brabazon successfully led the cam-paign for the Crown to ban outright all speaking of the Gaelic tongue in the entire province of Leinster.

He was shrewd at using Ireland to play the Crown for his own financial gain. By the will of his ambition, the Crown were forced to enact a policy of aggressive military advancement outwards from the Pale (Dublin) to 're-plant' Ireland. Which basically meant removing any and all hostile Gaels and appointing Braba-zon as landlord. At his height, he had landed interests in the counties of Dublin, Meath, Westmeath, Kildare, Louth, Down and Laois where I'm from. In 1545, he received a grant of one dissolved monastery that gave him possession of a whopping *forty-three townlands* across the counties of Meath and Louth.

So, this one self-serving accountant is a considerable por-tion responsible for the story of the Ireland that I grew up in. This man who treated Ireland like a giant bank account from which to withdraw as much money and land and influence as possible – and here I am, sitting in a cafe on a street in the Liber-ties which they named after him and his family. Of course, it's not that cut and dried, and the Brabazon descendants carried on owning the area for 300 years more and helped to shape its his-tory in different ways.

But knowing all this, it's hard not to feel that this story has been bubbling up through the cracks in the pavement for the past half millennium. Silently shaping how we perceive this space of ours and how we see ourselves in it.

And if the land beneath our feet can retain a certain memory, then it must follow that each occupied square foot of Earth possesses its own. A ghost of the accumulation of all the different things that happened on/in it. The pleasant and poisonous screams, the roaring pitch battles, and the moments when two people told each other they were in love. Does the ground keep a little piece of that for itself? Does space somehow contain infinite memory? Or maybe it's that the space that our space is occupying is in fact memory. Maybe every foundation we lay down, every bomb we detonate, every footstep, all pays into one big invisible 'data fabric'.

Like the ancient Greek philosopher Zeno and his 'paradox of place', which Samuel Beckett references heavily in his play *Endgame*. References lost on 99 per cent of the audience and a fair percentage of the cast, trust me.

Zeno's paradox of place states that if a grain of sand takes up a grain of sand's worth of space in our universe, then that space itself must also be taking up a grain of sand's worth of space somewhere else. That tiny space must be occupying its own space, and so on *ad infinitum*, therefore the universe is infinite.

Even the language of mathematics, the language we write to build computers and suspension bridges, does not describe a fixed 'place' in order to accurately mould our universe. It only describes possibility.

Now, I have heard tell of psychogeography enthusiasts who relate to the spaces around them differently by taking a map of Dublin, say, and navigating their way around Jakarta with it. Or, who throw dice at a crossroads to tell them where to go. A kind of chaos psychogeography.

A technique similar to the ancient (mainly) Chinese philosophy of the Tao where, when practitioners needed guidance for an important life decision, instead of going through the rigmarole of rationally reasoning through the different imagined futures, and weighing up the various pros and cons of how things *might* go based on a limited set of known variables, they would instead seek the right path by divining the intelligence of the universe. By drying out a tortoise shell, whacking it with a wooden mallet, and interpreting guidance from the patterns in the cracks.

In other words, throwing dice to tell them where to go. Not exactly an exact science, exactly.

Or the group the Situationist International, who emerged in Europe in the late 1950s, whose most prominent member was an author, filmmaker and theorist called Guy-Ernest Debord. He wrote a book called *The Society of the Spectacle*, a critique of capitalist urban life in which he describes how all utilitarian (functional-centric) society contributes to an increasing degree of fragmentation among its citizens. Big, productive cities, where modern manufacturing prevails, combined with its society's abstracted story of unity, which is passively consumed by the workers in some form or other, leads to the increasing atomisation of their lives and of society's life as a whole. And as such, the society's whole 'character' becomes reduced to that of spectacle – an image of an image of an image – a kind of simulacrum of itself, resulting in vast numbers of isolated city-dwelling people going around playing fake roles with each other, never being themselves and sleepwalking their way through their whole lives.

Together, the Situationists would embark on a *dérive* around the city of Paris. Long, aimless strolls, not motivated by work or an obligation to get anywhere. The only rule was that they were not to go the typical routes that the city was attempting to funnel them down, for example into commercial centres or towards sporting arenas.

Swinging from lampposts, sniffing shrubs and strolling by the light of the moon, these youngsters renounced fixed utilitarian capitalism and all of its monotony, to entertain the possibility of seeing their world differently. To see it anew, as a place to play freely and be spontaneous, in order to demonstrate how the spaces we occupy, and how we relate to them, inherently changes our behaviour. It changes our mood, our identities and ultimately our 'character' as a group.

I can relate to this notion of spectacle. In the past, in the middle of a fight or some other stressful situation, as a kind of defence mechanism, I can remember my perspective on reality shifting so that it felt more like I was watching a show of my own life. I demoted myself to an onlooker. A bystander one degree removed. A ticket-holder, as opposed to what I actually was: an active participant in the show.

I transformed pain into spectacle. Sometimes it was just easier that way.

The Dutch artist Constant was another leading light in the Situationist movement. Around that time in the late 1950s, what with all the new and exciting innovations going on in technological automation, with its near-limitless technocratic potential to provide everything humanity required, many Situationists were under the impression that in the future, people would have *a lot* more free leisure time.

Thus, the architecture that would be required for the future ought to reflect the most aspirational state of being that one can attain, namely the freedom to be creative and playful.

Buildings would not be bound to the ground at all, but instead would have flexibility to change. Like adjustable folding walls, malleable shapes, expanding floors and suspended rotating structures.

Constant's architectural project was called 'New Babylon'. A vast collection of maps, sketches, three-dimensional models and paintings that gave conceptual form to his future of human doings at play.

He wanted our societies to evolve creatively as well as technologically. In the rapidly emerging 'machine age', he wanted our spaces to more closely reflect the true nature of reality – changefulness. And to move away from the illusion that reality is permanent. Because I think, just like me, he felt disturbed by the fixed, utilitarian faux-permanence of city's designs.

The inflexible, immovable environment amounted to a feeling of spiritual decay. He should have got a job in film and television.

Constant's vision of the future pretty much sums up the environments in which I work. Inside the four walls of a studio, the shapes of the spaces (sets) they build and we occupy are constantly changing. That is one of the things I enjoy most about my work: its impermanence.

I love the idea of combining imagination and technology to transform our spaces to chime more harmoniously with the incurable 'movingness' of reality, so as to cultivate and support more collective joyful human states like creativity.

Changing one's place and how we relate to it keeps cropping back up in different forms. Like today, the Burning Man festival in Nevada is a Situationists' dry dream. Every year, a huge group of human doings get together in fabulously camp costumes to create lots of spontaneous situations by building Black Rock City:

> '... a temporary metropolis dedicated to community, art, self-expression, and self-reliance. In this crucible of creativity, all are welcome.'

Burningman.org

And all of this psychogeography, combined with my playful practice of expanding porousness, got me thinking about the space of my own bodymind. How I relate to it, and how the principles of psychogeography could be applied.

The other day, I bumped my head going down into a basement so hard that it bled. And after boring two or three other people with the little story of it and getting them to feel the bump and everything, it served as a reminder of how, alongside flesh and bone, first and foremost my body is a collection of stories. My body is as much an accumulation of stories as it is 'physical'. In the bodymind awareness, you can find the sensations of blood, flesh, bone and belief, like systemic layers. So, psychogeographically speaking, the stories that I tell (myself and others) about my own body, just like my fame story, occupy as much legitimate space and hold as much responsibility in the body as the bones that keep it upright.

Like the two brown moles on my left neck. And how I must always remember to protect them from the sun because I'm worried that they might become cancerous. As a kid, the doctor gave me a very po-faced warning about always keeping them covered, and by his tone I could tell that he had seen other coco-puffs just like mine turn red and nasty and grow tendrils.

Then, after that doctor's visit, we went off to Spain on holidays and I got burnt to a crisp.

Later, the coco-puffs were awarded a dramatic second act.

I was nineteen years old and in eastern Australia, having sex with a very charming German girl called Janna in the back of her van.

She dug a long, painted fingernail into my neck and tore one of the coco-puffs clean off.

And before I was aware that this had happened, before I saw any blood, I distinctly remember frowning down and wondering, 'Am I bleeding?' Before fountains worth sprang forth and gushed all over the place. All over her, her van, everything. Then, all woozy and naked and squirting blood, I staggered out of her curtained Volkswagen at nine o'clock in the morning onto a sandy suburban street with rows of houses either side, and fled into the house past my sleeping friend Brian and crumpled into his shower. Janna pursued close behind brandishing a bottle of disinfectant and apologising profusely.

After the bleeding finally settled, I was elated! Because she had saved me (half) the hassle of an unpleasant procedure, or so I thought. But my elations were premature. The coco-puff head grew back just as strong as ever after a week or two, which only confirmed my worst fear: that the surface of it is just the tip and, like the iceberg that felled the *Titanic*, the true menace lies below.

Other little tales like that hang off my body like moss growing all over. Old criticisms that have been there long enough to become comforts. Like my left jaw.

When I played Richard III in 2015, my hunch would have made Quasimodo blush. And the look came complete with the complementary withered left arm.

Spurred tirelessly on by the cattle prod of fear and self-doubt, I went around with a withered left arm, both at rehearsals and at home, all day every day for about eighteen weeks. And from the strain that caused in my shoulder, multiplied by all the maniacal on-stage shouting, it earned me some dysfunction in my temporo-mandibular joint (TMJ), the joint which connects the jaw to the skull. Just below my ear and behind the jawbone, there is a quite audible and strangely satisfying popping sensation.

In the morning, the sensation is like a warm blanket, since when I puff out my left cheek and it goes *pop!*, it feels good, and brings back memories of performing in that play.

Injuries often become big headline stories in the body. You often hear former sports athletes telling the stories of their bodies in this way. Some part of their anatomy that let them down through injury in the quest for what they knew they were capable of achieving.

I have had my fair share, like my right knee. Once, we were playing soccer in the front garden, and we put big grey cinderblocks down as goals. You know where this is going. I was the goalie, and was wearing those huge over-sized yellow goalkeeper's gloves that made me look like a deflated Disneyland mascot.

The ball came flying and I made a committed dive, and my knee landed square onto the jagged corner of the cinderblock and burst clean open. There was a ton of blood, and you could see bits you're not supposed to be able to see. The thick white scar still remains and reminds today, just below the kneecap.

Or my left ankle. Once I was among a bunch of actors in north London, and, as per usual, we hadn't warmed up properly for our weekly soccer game. We were having a kickaround on one of those artificial football pitches in the park with the high cage barriers all around. I came out the other side of a clumsy collision with the actor James McAvoy, and twisted my outer left ankle so badly that it made a loud cracking noise like a branch being snapped. He stopped, 'Whoa, that sounded bad – are you OK?' 'Sure,' I said, 'I'm grand. Just a sec . . .'

After limping off to the sidelines I rotated it and gave it a good wiggle, but the pain had quickly and completely subsided.

So, I gave a thumbs-up and leapt back to my feet and played on. I even scored a slick little volley before the adrenaline wore off and the true agony began to descend. My ankle swelled up to the size of a squash. And another actor, Steven Cree, had to carry me limping to his car and drive me the 300 metres home. After that, I avoided putting my full weight on that ankle for over a year, and didn't play soccer again for another six.

So, just by spending some time nestled in moviemeditation with some specific body parts, and noticing what memories/stories naturally emerge, I can't help but see how I relate to them.

What way I give them the word. And I can't help but notice how a common theme that occurs in the stories is injury, particularly down my left side. The conclusion I must deduct is that I believe on some level that my body is a liability. When it is also just as much of a fact that it is a great gift. It gets me around, protects me from harm, runs innumerable vital systems in the background so that I don't have to, knows how to recreate itself through cellular replication. My body is not a liability, it is a fucking miracle.

These stories that we tell ourselves, either consciously or unconsciously, are not to be overlooked in their power to guide the continuing story of our bodies.

And when we can see ourselves in this way, as a catalogue of stories with discernible themes, then it is also possible see how the stories are malleable and updateable. That it is possible to realign the story via other equally truthful themes to more of a balance between negativity and positivity. I am convinced that getting one's stories straight, if you will, improves the body's overall health.

By closing my eyes and getting nice and comfortable and settled in syrupy stillness, tuning deeply in to my body, I can take a little time to rebalance any overly negative, injury-laden body story by saying it a prayer. Showing my body some well-deserved, overdue gratitude, and in this way, just like the shakti, gratitude itself becomes an actual physical sensation.

A prayer to my body

Thanks, heart, for ceaselessly beating. What a miracle you are.

Thank you, nervous system, for the sensations of cold and heat on my skin, which wakes up all the little sleeping cardiovascular muscles who are responsible for opening and closing my veins.

Thank you, kidneys, for ceaselessly filtering.

And you, lungs, for continually proliferating oxygen through me.

Thank you, legs, for expertly walking me around.

And last but not least, thank you hips, despite the fact that ye are stiff bastards sometimes, thanks anyway for doing the best you can. You are the only hips I have, and intuitively I know that you are alerting me to the fact that there is some work that needs to be done on another muscle not pulling its weight in your locale (ass).

Amen.

Just like the Situationists, through looking closely at the story of my body without agenda, I can see and relate to myself anew.

With a little will, it's possible to discern where we might be perpetuating and worsening a needlessly negative inner narrative about something, and also it may be possible to rebalance the story by rebuilding its foundations in acceptance and gratitude. So that going forward, when we daydream, and our focus drifts naturally inwards, we are gifted as a bonus the physical sensation of gratitude.

The more of these negative stories we uncover, examine and recontextualise, stories that may have dug in and for a long time have gone unaddressed (that problematic lower back, that stiff neck and clicking jaw, that selfish brother, that melodramatic sister, that inconsiderate husband, or the 'how shitty it is to be me' narrative, etc.), the less rigid and fixed the world remains.

And now, a haiku:

A nudge of light force

Sends us back to the cradle,

Which catches our corpse!

Here is another useful little meditation technique, which is to do with interacting with the space around me. This one is particularly delicious when done in direct sunlight.

When we are sufficiently rested into the stillness, when we have reached a quiet platform of consciousness, now this may sound a tad science-fiction, but it becomes possible to *draw energy into* our bodies from the environment around us. It is possible to synthesise the shakti energy that is inherently crackling in the atmosphere all around.

Tai chi is a kind of practice of this. It works on a similar principle. Tai chi roughly translates to the 'supreme principle', and this is because it is the practice of uniting the body and mind together, while cultivating a deep sense of stillness in movement.

I was taught the basics of tai chi by an actor who came in to shoot for one day as a policeman with us on *Umbrella*. And after just ten minutes of practising together, I felt a significant increase in energy.

When we are deeply connected with our present environment, substantial shakti transfer becomes possible. And the more deeply we connect through ourselves, the more our environment gives us back in return.

Breathe in vagally, nutritiously, and speak the silent affirmation of the mantra:

I invite the energy of the whole world in. I absorb infinite energy into my core. I invite the crackling shakti in the ether all around to flow through me like a river.

Whatever the wording, as long as you mean it.

This allows the borders of your body's form to become porous, and eventually dissolve. Embracing it sends Mexican waves of light tingles across the surface of your skin, as this new energy comes cascading in through your pores.

I experience the results of this as euphoric, intense rushes of shakti. And as pleasurable contractions in my lower jaw, and tears welling up in my eyes. I feel every cell of my body fizzing and exploding and expanding. And it is so exhilarating and life-affirming, knowing that I can communicate with and harness this unknowably intelligent force at will.

It was through this technique that, while in a prolonged space voyage session, I first experienced the disappearance of my hands. When this happens, the sensation feels like they have been removed from the field of form. It is like handing them back to god. Now my disappearing hands have become a milestone of having arrived at a certain platform of consciousness.

Thank you for the healing,

And bless you for this feeling,

That sends the tears a-streaming

Down what used to be my face.

Dramatic Pause

⁓

In the art of acting, I'm convinced that stillness is the secret that's dying to be told.

The essential job of acting is to act natural while watching yourself. This is at the heart of the actor's job, and yet it is the thing that actors have the most trouble with (me, for example): acting natural while having to watch yourself acting natural.

For me, because I initially approached acting from a social perspective, my focus was less absorbed in honouring the fictional world we were occupying, and more absorbed in coping with the uncomfortable feeling of being watched.

And sometimes, when I felt I'd finally done enough practice and preparation, I'd get over it and then love the feeling of being watched. It was comparable to, after a long and painful period of doubt-plagued failure, finally being able to do quadratic equations in school. Like there was a strong, soothing safety net of experience under me now, which made me feel larger than myself. But other times, the feeling of being watched made me shrink with nerves.

And what caused this discomfort was not being watched, but my *knowing* that I was being watched. And this knowing was what caused me to become self-aware – in other words, to start closely watching myself. And it was this close watching, and subsequent over-correction of myself, that was the source of my discomfort.

What is the practice of sitting in stillness if not becoming more adept at closely watching yourself? This is one of the big reasons why, in acting, the practice of meditation is the secret that is dying to be told.

Initially, as a young'un, I unconsciously decided that when it came time to act, my efforts were best put into learning how to mask my acute self-awareness.

Acting was not about confronting the fear I was feeling, but suppressing it well. I believed that when one got past all the theoretical waffle and right down to where the rubber meets the road, the real (yet secret) work of the actor was to continue enduring all the anxiousness and nervousness before an audition or during a scene or whatever (obviously there was nothing to be done about that), but to become adept at concealing its external effects. Anxiety was not to be invited in and nurtured; it was to be rejected and left out in the cold.

I wonder, if someone had told me at the time that I was going about it in exactly the wrong way, could I have done anything to change it?

Sometimes before an audition I would be shitting myself, quite literally. In the bathroom coping with nerves intense enough to loosen my stool. Paper towelling under my sweaty arms and tweaking my appearance in the mirror while quietly trying to talk my inner jumper down off his ledge. Then, strolling into the audition room, script pages in hand and heart racing, all 'Hi, hello', trying my best to look relaxed. The performance itself came secondary to all this in terms of time and effort spent worrying.

It got to where I would try anything I could to beat the stomach-churning nerves. These auditions were often conducted in tiny little rooms in central London, and I would come in and immediately start doing little laps around the room while carrying on the chit-chat with the confused casting director. Visiting all four corners of the tiny space in an effort to expand it, and feel like I 'owned' it, while I was in there. That worked surprisingly well sometimes.

Luckily, there was also the occasion when the stars aligned and the mists of anxiety miraculously parted, and I would wriggle free enough that the audition ended up more closely resembling my first ever religious baptism. The dragon I spent my young life pursuing.

In a way, acting was like a volatile gamble. Since those few victories justified the numerous losses, even if the victories didn't result in me getting the part. Reliving the feeling, and finding freedom from myself in the audition room environment, was the holy grail. That was the end, not the means.

And then, the delicious icing on the cake was that 'you got the job' feeling. Hearing that would be enough to have me levitating a foot off the floor for three days.

For me, because my childhood anxiety was all bound up with needing to be liked, as an adult this translated into needing to get hired.

And this unquenchable need provided the bulletproof motivation to keep going no matter what.

Once, I was twenty-one-ish and had made the pilgrimage out to Los Angeles in search of great success. And after a full day's slew of racing around town doing 'generals' with casting directors, my final one for the day was an audition for a role in some Jack Black movie. I was ushered into a coldly lit room by the warm and friendly tones of three casting ladies.

They flattered me with unexpected compliments, and told me they'd seen some of my stuff and thought I would be *great* for the part.

'So, whenever you're ready!' Which prompted the tired, skinny guy with the ponytail behind the camcorder to click the button, and on popped the little red light, and I did . . . something. I couldn't tell you exactly what it was, but the ladies instantly all burst out laughing. But not the warm kind of laughter one hopes to receive, more of a callous, career-ending laughter. And then one of them shushes the other two and gets herself together enough to hold up a hand like you would to a recalcitrant dog, 'Stop, stop. You're not *actually* going to do it like that, are you?'

'Ummm . . .'

I sloped back to the parking lot feeling a kind of vague, far-away numbness. Here I was, 5,000 miles from home, feeling like I had absolutely no idea what I was doing, 'but screw it all anyway because it doesn't matter that much . . .'

I had been outed as the ridiculous, talentless moron I secretly suspected I always was underneath all the brash front.

My agent called: 'How'd it go?' When I told him, he took pity on me by sending me back across town to a warehouse declaring, 'Robbie, they will give you some cool free clothes.'

When I got there, I was greeted by two attractive young blonde women standing on a raised platform behind a big black countertop which went up past my chest and made me feel like a little boy.

They gave me two pairs of blue jeans that were so wide they looked like they'd been tailored to fit Mr Squary from the Mr Men collection. As I thanked them and made to leave, having left what I felt was an adequately cool impression, I turned on my heel and promptly marched full-speed into the glass front door. I whacked my nose so hard that the whole building shook. The stars in my vision faded just enough to turn around and catch the two girls behind the counter doubled over in laughter, wiping the tears off their scrunched up faces. And oddly, at no point that whole day did it occur to me to consider other, less excruciating forms of employment.

Michael Ironside told me that in the Japanese tradition of theatre, when approaching how to act a scene, one first identifies the obvious emotional route through it, then flips it 180 degrees, and then begins.

So, for example, where you'd find obvious happiness, you invite the possibility of sadness. Where boredom is obvious, one seeks excitement. Joy suggests despair, and so on. Just like in the *Tao Te Ching*. The perfect approach for a contrarian such as I.

So, in the spirit of my board-treading brothers and sisters in Japan, I decided to flip it, and ponder how being an actor has improved my practice of movementlessness. Just to see where things end up.

Before going on this journey, I never realised how acting is in itself a kind of dynamic form of meditation.

Let me set the scene.

On the morning of filming, we the actors are driven to the unit base of the production. A circus-worth of double-banger trailers, with labels clinging to their doors in plastic laminate sleeves, like 'Hair', 'Makeup', 'Director', 'Stunts', 'AD' and so on. On *Umbrella*'s unit base, the actor's trailers had to have codename labels on them to confuse would-be stalkers. My most recent one was 'Punk Panther'.

After a half-hour's fannying around for breakfast – 'Morning! Morning! Morning!' – then it's into hair and makeup. Most makeup trailers are heaving with floor-to-ceiling plastic storage boxes and shelves chock-full of cosmetic products, and extremely brightly lit vanity mirrors lining the far wall. I always request that they cover the mirror I'm sitting in front of with a piece of whiteboard, because there's nothing more natural than having to stare at yourself for half an hour before shooting, just in case you weren't feeling self-aware enough.

Then, once teeth are brushed and whiskers trimmed, it's across to the studio to be 'wired', meaning a sound technician cleverly hides a mobile microphone somewhere on your person. This was a task made extra difficult by Klaus's very revealing ensembles.

On *Umbrella*, you feel like a member of the G8 summit walking around the lot with the level of security detail.

Once the studio bloodlight goes off we enter, and inside, despite the darkness, the big room is alive with energy. Hundreds of crew members milling back and forth, murmuring good mornings at each other, scurrying from A to B, all different departmental universes existing in parallel.

In adjacent studio spaces, you can hear the shrill trills of power drills and clanking of wood staplers echoing across from the carpenters on some other half-built set. On the live set, you're drawn like a moth towards the glare of enormous movie lights catching the wafting atmospheric smoke, a potentially lethally poisonous gaseous expression of glycerin deployed to soften the edges of the HD image and fill the frame with texture. And as the actors wander onto set one by one, costumes half on, coffee cups in hand and heads down, murmuring into their scripts, the assistant director shoos all the crew technicians away to make space for 'blocking'. Blocking means a rehearsal of the scene we're about to

shoot with just the director and actors, with the intention of fielding questions, overcoming all physical and mental roadblocks,
embarking on miniature rewrites, coming up with alternate little
improvs for shits and giggles, all so as to put a finer point on the
scene. Apart from logistically complicated set pieces, this is typically the only time a cast and their director get to rehearse the
scene before shooting. Then, once everyone is happy enough
with the size and shape, the crew technicians wander back in to
watch the crew blocking rehearsal. And once that's all nice and
done, the actors pass the relay baton over to 'second team'. Second
team are a group of stand-ins of a similar size and colour to the
cast, so that the cinematographer and director can position them
while tweaking the lighting. Second team are a luxury only found
on the larger-budget stuff.

And as we all hurtle towards the first shot of the day, all energies nearing fever pitch, as a team of hundreds scramble to make
double sure that they're not going to be the one individual who
fucks things up and stalls proceedings.

Then, out of all that chaos, the first AD shouts 'Roll sound!'
and a *cacophonous* silence suddenly drops over us all like an invisible fire blanket. To where you could hear a mouse let one go.
Two hundred-odd people, who had just been beavering away at a
dull roar, freeze like mannequins, and as a result of this, the whole
set becomes very, very charged with the energy of possibility. It's a
do-or-die highwire energy, borne out of the extraordinary balanc-
ing act now happening across an imperceivably complex network
of technicians and machinery.

This energy is magic, and creates the perfect conditions for
an actor to negotiate with their fear.

Because if this moment is not feeling good for you, and the
scene feels deader than a doornail, and you secretly suspect that it

is you who is the one killing it, then it becomes vitally critical to tune in to see what is going on and see if you can't find a way to untangle that knot.

In the before times, when I had less experience, this energy was a source of nerves and anxiety as well as excitement. I was addicted to it, addicted to trying to conquer it, but I was also afraid of it. I used to think that being afraid of it was the reason why I was so drawn to it, like I had to continuously re-slay the dragon over and over again to prove something to myself outwardly that I could not give to myself inwardly. Again, like learning how to be a social person in a group as a kid, performance came parcelled up with fear which had to be managed and concealed.

In lieu of trust in myself, and trust that the moment always provides if you let it, the kind of trust required to relax into my natural ability and spontaneity, I opted for the controlling approach. In a bid not to be smothered by the pressure of this moment, I'd have to have it all plotted out in my head quite rigidly in advance. This created an excessive glass ceiling which limited the overall flexibility, both physical and emotional, of the performance. I am in love with acting, and as such, I am a bit fascist about it. And for me, movies and TV shows are often spoiled before they have a chance to get off the ground by those in my vocation who cannot relax into the moment fully while the camera is rolling. Who cannot allow themselves to respond spontaneously in this moment, and trust themselves to just let it be. So to conceal this inner mistrust, they seek sanctuary in old tropes, like doing an impression of that raspy Clint Eastwood movie voice (not Clint himself, though – he's the business), or looking really serious all the time. Nothing conveys weakness quite like an actor assuming a serious pose. Seriousness in acting, I've found, is a response to the pressure of the actor's real environment – the lights, intimidating machinery and many-eyed crew technicians – not the imaginary world they are supposed to be occupying.

It is the emotional equivalent of being stranded on a tiny desert island, unable to move for fear of drowning.

I remember a defining lightbulb moment when I found myself in this situation while playing Richard III. It was during the curse of Queen Margaret, the hateful widow of the murdered Henry VI, who is reduced to depending on the charity of her husband's murderers to get by.

Joely Richardson, our Margaret, was catapulting fire at me across the stage, but I was too busy trying to act offended and act scandalised and act serious for the benefit of the audience. I felt obliged to be always expressing something. Giving the audience their money's worth by narrowing eyes/glaring/scoffing/pouting/pursing/furrowing/frowning/biting lips/clenching teeth/clenching hands/clenching neck/clenching shoulders. Et cetera . . .

And all this unnecessary acting layer that I was lacquering on was the thing that was making the scene feel awful and artificial for me. But then, the pressure of the awfulness built to a critical point and I finally caved, and a little voice popped up inside and nudged me: 'Stop it! Stop fucking *acting*, and just listen to Margaret. *Listen* to what she is saying, damn you!' Now, this may seem obvious, simply listening to what is being said to you, but when acting in the contrived atmosphere of a theatre or a set, sometimes it is easy to forget. After that, the play became a transcendent joy, because I had (re)found sanctuary in listening.

This is why good acting is in itself a kind of dynamic form of meditation.

The actor Ron Perlman once told me that he acted alongside a surrogate nephew/son of Marlon Brando called Eddie, and while they were on set he asked, 'Hey, did you ever get any good acting advice from him?' And Eddie told Ron that Marlon said, right before a take was about to happen, 'I check my asshole.' Marlon tuned in with his asshole, and if it was puckered tight, it probably wasn't going to be a good take. But if it was nice and relaxed, it probably would be a good take.

Perhaps he was being a mite facetious about it, but Marlon was still advising a bodyscan. There is method in this madness, and not just for acting. Situating one's being in the lower torso is to relinquish ego control and re-embrace spontaneity. It instructs the nervous system to relax, which regulates heartbeat and hormones, soothes the mind and lowers stress. So for each take, Marlon had something clearer and more natural to give.

Nowadays, when that electric moment of possibility descends, there is nothing more thrilling than being prepared enough to be able to listen to the languageless part of my consciousness, and know that it always has an infinitely better next move in mind than I could've come up with, and my trust being rewarded. This is a wonderful, exciting, confidence-building, infinitely consistent safety net.

That is how meditation has benefitted my work, and it is a significant thing.

In the times wrought with indecision, in times of doubt, just by relinquishing control and resting back into the natural flow of flowfulness, and accepting the nerves, and allowing for the excitement, boredom, joy, madness, any emotion that wants to take the spotlight, I know that I will be guided in an interesting and spontaneous direction. For me, this is what it means to negotiate with fear and trust in the power of the universe.

When I realised that it was way more important in acting to be relaxed and listening (both to myself and others) than to be 'in control', a lightbulb went on in (not above) my head.

It gave me eyes to see much more of the default movement settings that were running in me while I was typically away, absorbed and distracted, pretending somewhere else. I learned that accepting the inevitability of thoughts coming in and out, as they tend to do, is to dismantle their power to be so disruptive. There are still anticipatory nerves as I prepare to play a role, of course, but relating to them differently through practice of meditation liberated me a great deal, and made my job more fun and less filled with aniticipatory dread. Mad to think, how something that seemed so minor was having such a major effect.

There is another concept in Japanese theatre called *ma*. *Ma* sort of means 'emptiness', but more an emptiness that is filled with possibility. I have also heard it translated into English as 'pregnant emptiness'. To create *ma* on the actor's face is to give the audience the opportunity to fill it in with their own projections.

Sometimes the absence of a reaction is a far stronger decision, demonstrating how, despite what's happening around them, the character has some emotional gravity of their own. It demonstrates a respect shown by the actor towards their character if they are not 'losing it' every five minutes, bouncing around like an emotional pinball. It's hard to respect a real person who is constantly emotionally hijacked by what other people say and what's happening around them, and it's difficult to care for someone who is never moved at all.

Lack of stillness, or an overly posed stillness, suggests to me someone who never learned to maturely deal with their own emotions.

It was fascinating discovering this concept, because *ma* might as well be another euphemism, like 'meditation', for stillfulness, except in the context of acting. In a deep creamy session of restful stillfulnessness, one is filling up their form with the emptiness that is rich with possibility. Ma is the onomatopoeic sound of a gentle exhale, and also *ohm* backwards, basically. In fact, this whole section could be entitled ma, as it is all about the benefits of finding stillness while performing.

Once thoughts were less of an obstacle, once I was nice and pregnant with the rich emptiness of *ma*, only then did it become possible to begin embracing the technique of 'sensualisation' (for want of a nicer-sounding word).

With space enough earned, I could start exploring by conjuring to mind, with my eyes open, say, an image, aroma, sound or taste. And I could consciously fill that rich space of *ma* without so much as moving a muscle. The imagination is a muscle, the memory is too. And when given regular exercise, the dynamism and range of pictures, sounds and sensations one can conjure up improves.

This is similar to an acting technique taught in the Stanislavski method called 'sense memory', where the actor recalls memories from their real life in order to relive them emotionally.

Substantial activity behind settled eyes is very interesting to watch. We can easily discern when an actor is thinking as opposed to thinking nothing.

Practising being comfortably still improved my ability to do this. It is a dimension that opens up and gives the actor infinite indoor space in which to play.

Like, for example, if I am in a riot scene, I may choose to conjure to mind the image of floating serenely over the surface of a misty mountain lake at dawn.

Nowadays, this is where the spiciness of acting lies. In finding the most honest, yet uniquely subtextual route below whatever is being said on the surface.

Acting is just like cake-making: it's about how to get adventurous with the layers.

'What was said that wasn't said was said
beneath what was said.'

Me

Then the challenge becomes how to quantum-leap from one
emotion to quite another, all the while smoothing out the edges
of the transitions. All the while remaining loyal to telling the story
you're telling. This is what I call the actor's dimension.

Fathoms below the writing is the actor's dimension, and it is
limitless in choice. It is the feeling dimension beneath the saying
dimension.

In the actor's dimension, just like the principle in Japanese
theatre, the actor is freed from responding predictably, and can be
reincarnated into another thought/feeling/reaction altogether.

That is the true juice. When I see an actor make an unexpected
turn, one emotion following another which, in my experience, has
never before accompanied that sequence of actions/words.

Like Anthony Hopkins's character, Stevens, in *The Remains
of the Day*. Stevens is a man who is saying one thing, almost
robotically, while the whole rest of his being is saying something
completely else.

Making the most of the actor's dimension is the difference
between watching a performance that is mediocre, and one that is
magical.

So how then to discover the most honest, yet unique route
through this dimension? Where and how to look for such an
intangible thing?

Well, one way is to create memories. I am much less into using my own.

To create, and then ultimately 'relive' memories and stories from the imagination is to begin to live the life of the character both inside and out. And to bring the life that was already being lived before the story begins very much into the story.

This way, the actor is part writer, part private eye and part psychologist. Memory is the invisible glue that bonds a whole life together, or, in some cases, tears it apart.

And no (wo)man is an island, but they are a citadel, with many rooms full of old dusty storage boxes, and one's character ought be treated just the same.

I ask the character all sorts of questions about his life, things that may not seem to have any direct bearing on the story. Favourite hobbies, political leanings, past loves? Greatest fears, hopes and dreams, shady finances. Allergies? Anything and everything – all of it helps to find things out about how he really feels in certain situations. And then, he'll start to surprise me. I experimented with this a lot when researching the character of Klaus for *The Umbrella Academy*.

Here are a couple of choice examples of mind-spew I wrote while journaling as Klaus around that time:

13/9/18

I have this voice in my head, which ... drives me forward. Keeps me going on. I know I can rely on it when I feel strange or weak. But now ... even that voice is falling apart. It's disintegrating. He's shrinking and it's harder to find him in there among all the others. I think it's time away from Dave, who smashed the way things were in there before anyway. But it's fine, it's just another turn of the page in the book. I mean, I don't know if the book is falling closed or turning forward, I can't tell, but the page is turning.

Definitely. And I'm scared that the next part will be more painful than the last.

And I'm scared that the pain will be for nothing, and I'll never get to the end.

That I'm in an endless tumble dryer/tombola/concrete mixer of pain-laden life that I can never get out of.

It's not that death scares me, it's that life carries on and on. I mean in this form, I've got great hair and a relatively controversial fashion sense.

I'm just so scared of having to start over.

10/1/21

Laugh out all the maddening pain. The pain tickles! It turns me on. I have no reservations in saying that and I'll say it to the rest of them because why should I carry it around like a leaden weight by myself? I have thought about Dad saying mean stuff to get me over the sexy line. When the drugs have flagged my dick, and the cult members keep fucking too fast, all impatient, I have conjured up Dad calling me a mistake and a failure, just to make it over the line. Dad's rejection is a sex aid, therefore

Dad is a sex toy. Ha-ha! How funny, and a turn-on all at
the same time. I would tell him, if I thought he would take
it the right way, but I know if I tried to pay him that
compliment he would scowl at me. Ironically, worsening
the problem!

Practising prolonging purposelessness first really helped to steady
my mind enough to be able to create clearer memories. Deep
down in the subcutaneous layers of consciousness, the imagination can run far wilder and freer. And forge many unexpected
connections, and then chronicle all that idea-flavoured honey as
it distils down into awareness.

The more memories I fill up Klaus's life with, the easier it is
to feel relaxed while walking around in his pointy boots. The
more that past events actively inform the present, the fuller he
feels. And the easier it is to trust him, and for it to become second
nature for him to trust me.

Recently, I performed in the play *Endgame* by Samuel Beckett.

It was originally written in French as *Fin de partie*, and then
premiered in London at the Royal Court Theatre in 1957, still in
French. What a topsy-turvy world. It is a surreal, clownish, existential one-act gallop all set in one dimly lit grey room with two
small windows and four strange characters. Outside their windows, you get the sense that the rest of the world has long since
been destroyed. Hamm sits in a wheelchair in the centre of the
stage, blindly blowing his dog whistle and barking orders and

abuse at Clov (me), who might be his son. Or who might have been a little boy that Hamm rescued long ago from the apocalyptic wastes. Nagg and Nell are Hamm's extremely old, legless, starving parents, who he keeps alive in two trashcans by feeding them a rare biscuit.

Rehearsals were four joyous weeks of pondering how to plot the most interesting and surprising route through the actor's dimension. And *Endgame* is the perfect playground for this, because although its themes are dark, it wholly embraces levity through clowning. Lots of horsing around, slapstick gags and physical comedy. There is also some direct communication with the audience. And no one really knows for sure what the fuck's going on anyway, so there's loads of space to play around in.

In our rehearsal room (which was less a room and more a womb), endless theories were bandied around as to what *Endgame* really 'means'. Through the wafting incense, we all slung theories across the table ranging from kitchen-sink to sci-fi. One theory that Frankie Boyle, our Hamm, proffered was that the entire play is symbolic of one brief moment in time taking place in the very last breath of a man's life. That *Endgame* is a ninety-ish-minute analogous depiction of his very last second before passing away, as he clings desperately to a life that will inevitably leave him. And all of his experiences and pain and joys are jumbling around in a tombola drum, as he struggles in vain to put some sort of shape on things, to establish a proper narrative, a respectable legacy in a tidy chronology, so that the journey through this human psyche can have the sensation of meaning something and making 'sense'. He clings to the last scraps and bits that he can remember, unable to just let it all go and pass peacefully into the white light that has been progressively overwhelming the darkness of his blindness as the play staggers towards its end(?).

'The end is in the beginning and yet
you go on.'

Hamm, *Endgame*

In the rehearsal room, we explored our characters, ourselves, the play and each other through yoga, trust exercises, prolonged sessions of unbroken eye contact, movement mirroring and emotional memory recreation games.

It was part rehearsal, part psychoanalysis. We recounted early childhood memories of times when we were overwhelmed by certain emotions, like shock, or embarrassment, or joy.

For shock, I told the story of when I was about nine years old, and my pal Phillip and I were mooching around in the local graveyard. I hunkered down in the sun next to a low rock wall to get a closer look at what a load of bees were swarming around, but I couldn't see what it was that was attracting their interest. So I shouted out to Phil, 'Look at all these fuckin' bees!', and from out behind the other side of the low rock wall, a strange man in a broad-brimmed green hat suddenly emerged, eyes bulging, and mockingly parroted, 'Bees!' I got such an intense fright I've never run so fast my whole life since. This grown man had hidden himself behind that wall, crouched like a coiled spring, waiting for the right moment to spring out and scare the life out of two unsuspecting children. And in the rehearsal room, I cannot describe the surreality of seeing the three other wonderful actors re-enacting a clownish, wordless recreation play of this longheld memory. It was touching.

Seán McGinley, our Nagg, the legless father who peers out of a trashcan like a sinister *Sesame Street* character next to his poor wife Nell, recollected this:

When I was about eleven or twelve, we were playing a game of football on the green in our estate. There was a heavy tackle and the lad I tackled didn't take it so well. So he picked up a small rock and threw it at me. Missed. So I picked up the nearest thing to me – a stick or branch type thing and threw it at him, and hit him on his head near his eye, so he claimed. He made a meal out of it and ran home screaming like a big baby. Couple hours later yer man's father arrives at our front door and recounts the whole story, saying his poor son was in bits at home. So my father said, 'That's terrible', and went into the living room and came back out with this lamp that had a water-mill scene painted on it, and when you switched it on, the heat from the bulb made this mechanism thing move and gave the illusion that the water was flowing over the water mill.

'Tell your son to look at the lamp and it will make his eye better', says my father.

'Thanks, John', says yer man's father. And off he went!

Afterwards, after he'd recounted this to us and watched it be recreated by three clowns, he said that a whole flood of old/new memories to do with that memory emerged. What he could initially remember was just the tip of the iceberg. He had not revisited the memory in a long time, and when he did, it yielded far more than what was visible on the surface.

Before we began the show's run, I made sure to practise some awareness while walking around the stage of the empty theatre. Back and forth, limping around in circles, re-treading the route of the play, facing out into the auditorium in every conceivable direction while visualising the audience-to-be, the many faces of the packed-out house. All the while staying present with(in) myself, scanning and observing what feelings drifted up inside. Keeping a keen (third) eye out for subtly limiting irrational fears, stubborn social conditionings, unhelpful little self-inflicted pokings that ran contrary and upstream to what we'd been preparing for weeks to achieve. Because:

'We create so much of our own trouble.'

Mooji

In this case meaning that now I had the play learned off, the final obstacle to overcome was myself. And when a sensation of inhibition emerged, likely inherited from a time in the past when I'd felt nervous standing in front of people, or felt acute disappointment at how my appearance in front of people had gone, I gave the sensation a new, present instruction. I conjured to mind every single line of the play to demonstrate fully to the old fear what new permissions it would be required to give.

When I felt a fearful inhibition arise as a result of trying out a line in a different way, I would interpret it as an invitation, not a deterrent, and lean directly into exactly what it didn't want me to lean into.

Inner sensation (past): I feel scared! I can't face *directly* out into the audience without looking away for that long during this bit.

Present: OK, I hear you. But there is nothing to fear. Let's try it. See? That wasn't so bad. We didn't die.

And as the old inhibition washed through me like a wave, it signified that the new present instruction had been received. The intent being that when we got out there and up and running, and I found myself standing in a certain spot, the old subtle fear had now been replaced by a new freedom. Which awarded me a greater dimension of free will, so that I could scream as loud as I wanted or deliver a line as directly to the audience as I chose, or eyeball them for as long as I liked while feeling free as a bird.

An audience hasn't bought tickets to come and see some actors on stage indulgently battling their own nerves.

As the spiritual teacher Sean Connery once sagely remarked, 'You can't be afraid to make a cunt of yourself.'

Old fears are stubborn, though, and require vigilance and occasional maintenance. I've noticed when a stage fear is deep enough set, it is perfectly possible for the sensation to return and for its influence to re-establish itself, necessitating a little further loving instruction.

Present: Fear, I feel you. But what have you been told, yes? Thank you.

Not always as easily said as done, but to be present is to see one's own performance fears less as something to run away from, and more as opportunities for discovery. Pushing through their barriers, hurtling head-on into that paralysing feeling in a performance always leads somewhere more interesting. And if I push through that feeling even just once on stage, then forevermore I possess a greater will to pursue my *own* path through the actor's dimension unencumbered – no matter if it occasionally wants to turn me through some thorny brambles. And I have become that bit more able to discern where the path gets shrouded by what I think other people think, because 99 per cent of what I think other people think is in my head.

Samuel Beckett was not a man to overshare when it came to the press; he even once famously gave a mute interview for Swedish television where he just stood stock-still on a hotel balcony near the sea and allowed them to film him. But once, he did let slip how his mission as a writer in the post-modern era was 'to depict no things'.

And in the very final words of his novel *Watt* he writes, 'No symbol where none intended.'

From that one might be tempted to deduct that every 'thing' – person, word, object – in his worlds is not a real thing, but symbols of a deeper reality.

And with little shadow of doubt I'd speculate that he suffered from frequent bouts of self-talk, with such quotes as:

> 'In me there have always been two fools, among others, one asking nothing better than to stay where he is and the other imagining that life might be slightly less horrible a little further on.'
>
> Samuel Beckett, *Molloy*

Ha! Tell me about it, Sam. And, like us all to some degree, he must have been mystified by the inner noise of it all. He was forged in a culture of academia, which lionised men with ordered minds, who fixed the world in concrete and kept it held there via unobjectionable 'laws'.

And all of this got me contemplating the nature of symbols, like the Arabic number 3. The number 3 written down is two swoops which meet in the middle, one on top of the other, like a pair of sideways boobs with no nipples. Two little squiggles combined on a page ingrain themselves so deeply in the collective psyche as to symbolise not one object, not two objects, but specifically three objects. But these three objects don't even have to all be the same object. You can have two chickens and a hamster, for example, and correctly say, 'I have 3 animals.' These objects could also be part of one object with three different components, for example, 'Recently, I was present at the birth of 3 alpacas all born conjoined together in one malformed body.'

Apologies for that image, but I was scarred from watching the movie *Colour Out of Space*, starring Nicolas Cage and Joely Richardson, a disturbing horror film in which some alpacas get fused together into a big blob. I once worked with Cage on a film. And on one very dark night, swaddled in our bulky medieval leathermail costumes, huddled around a gas-powered heater outside Kreuzenstein Castle in Austria, Nick turned to me wide-eyed and serious and enquired, 'What do you know about the mysticism of leprechauns?'

And looking back, I wish I'd had more to say. I wish I could've told him more about the different symbolic forms leprechauns have taken since we began to notice them in Ireland. Or told him the spooky story of the púca, a ghost that stalks the land who has been known to take the form of a four-legged creature and steal newborn babies by mounting them up on its back. Or the fact that *as Gaeilge* (in the Irish language), the symbol for a gust of wind is *sí gaoithe* which, when translated literally, means the sensation of an invisible entity or entities, like leprechauns or fairies, scurrying swiftly by.

Or the word *alltar*. I love the word *alltar*, because it refers to the whole invisible aspect of the world. *Alltar* is that which is there but cannot be directly perceived on our limited bandwidth of consciousness, like a leprechaun. *Alltar* is a humbling notion, because it encapsulates that which is eternally concealed to us behind an imperceivable veil that, through our limited sensory windows, we cannot reach.

'Our physical bodies occupy the *ceantar*
[the opposite of *allltar*, meaning a place,
region or province] but our minds can easily
slip into the *allltar*.'

Manchán Magan

The symbology of leprechauns is rich because it comes from a language made of magical concepts, deeply interwoven with how people in Ireland perceived the elements of the world around them.

But back at Kreuzenstein Castle, sitting in the warming tent, I was twenty years old and yet knew none of this. The only presence of a magical leprechaun in my upbringing was a chubby little stuffed toy with a ginger beard and a hat on, and when you squeezed his belly he did an instrumental version of 'When Irish Eyes Are Smiling'.

And no symbolism of the like was given remotely enough seriousness to be taught to us alongside the Irish language. The meaning of what Irish words symbolised was taught by translating them directly into English words. They seemed more concerned with teaching us how to write in perfect grammar before being able to either speak or understand it.

So, as a result, the symbol I had in my wheelhouse of leprechauns for Nick was the same one that he had – the corporatised version with the ginger sideburns. The mascot in the green suit that you'd be likely to see on the front of a diabetes-inducing cereal box if you'd accidentally wandered down the wrong aisle. The leprechaun was taken, and reassigned as a symbol of the marketplace.

So I said, 'Pff . . . I don't know, Nick. Ah . . . only that they have pots of gold at the end of the rainbow and ride around on sheep, and wear little green suits and hats.'

And he replied in earnest, '. . . because I think my assistant, Michael, might be a leprechaun.'

His assistant, Michael, was diminutive in stature, slight of shoulder, and from the UK.

I said, 'Why? Because he's a small gentleman?'

'Yeah, that, and also because he was a mysterious, abandoned baby who was found in a basket on the steps leading up to somebody's front door in London. So, I wonder if god hasn't put him in my path to hire him because he's a leprechaun?'

Afterwards, when I retold that story, I balked at how far Nick's head seemed to be up in the clouds, but today I find his curiosity admirable. His imagination enviable.

And also, it's a little saddening how my own culture was taught to me in such a shallow way, and mostly known only via the broken telephone of another larger, more capitalistic culture.

But I feel grateful too, because if it is at all possible to go and pay a visit to the *alltar*, the hinterlands of consciousness, where the leprechauns come from, then the practice of sitting in sub-lime spaciousness is just the vehicle to take me there.

Nowadays, the number 3 has been reassigned to do many different jobs, and woven into many different contexts. It can represent part of a coded sequence designed to encrypt a piece of information, or be the spine of the typical story structure, or be magic like in that annoying song, or it can be used to patch through a phone call. It can be a harbinger of bad luck, or a harbinger of good luck, or a symbol that represents the never-ending Hindu lifecycle of *samsara*. So the more you focus in on the symbol 3, the more stories you discover hanging off it like moss, and the less easy it is to pin down what it essentially means. As civilisations have overthrown one other, so too have they remixed, reused and recontextualised existing symbols like 3 over and over again to guarantee majority recognition and workable function of whatever shared thing the 3 has been attached to.

And 3 is one of the simpler ones. What happens when we call to mind symbols like 'eternity'? Or 'death'? These are also symbols, because in lieu of them actually happening, they occur as self-generated concepts in our interior and as words in our exterior.

In modern discourse, sometimes it feels like we have exchanged our true reality for the shallower, arbitrary symbols of reality. As though the symbols themselves are given greater importance over and above their meaning. But the problem with this is no matter what we are told, if we haven't experienced it for ourselves, we are always only imagining it, so we don't really experience the truth of what the symbolic reality is trying to convey, we only experience our own symbolic versions of it. We are only ever experiencing our own selves.

Twice winner of the Pulitzer Prize, journalist Walter Lippmann once shouted at me across a public swimming pool: 'The only feeling that anyone can have about an event he does not experience is the feeling aroused by his mental image of that event.'

I was not a pessimistic child by any means, but when it came to school lessons, I always felt that for me, they were defined not by what they contained, but by what they lacked. And I could never quite put my finger on why . . . What it was that was missing.

I just had this intuition that there was something right at the centre of a target somewhere else, which school felt more like a distraction from. And I watched other cleverer, more devoted students passing through whose passion I craved, whose passion I wanted to emulate, but I could never drum up the motivation.

The mire of futility towards the classroom lessons emanated from a deep place, a place I could never quite put into wordzzzz.

The philosopher Alfred North Whitehead once tapped this into the back of my head in Morse code: 'In the Garden of Eden, Adam saw the animals before he named them. In the traditional system, children name the animals before they see them.' Intuitively, it was this paradox that I was sensing, but I had no language for it yet. And the paradox was this: that school attempted to teach us about the world almost exclusively through words, numbers and other symbols (not including PE, of course; or PT, as my Dad calls it). In school, learning the symbolic version of stuff was put on a level of equal importance to actually experiencing stuff.

On one of the class's blackboards, there were symbols the same as our language denoting another language. On another, there were symbols further broken down into their composite parts and grammar. On another, the same symbols were used to indicate events in contemporary history. On another, they used the same symbols to represent the mechanics of reality. Numbers with arrows next to diagrams. Words stacked upon words in copy books underlined smartly in red pen.

To me, it felt like the code was being given us not as symbolic of the universe, but as the actual fabric of the universe.

And the ability to regurgitate all of the symbols in the right order was what was given the utmost reward in our reality. But with no real knowledge of what these symbols were actually referring to, the words and numbers were brittle things, easily broken and forgotten about. It was only the rare teacher who had the passion to inspire enough empathy in me so that I felt like I was also really experiencing what I was learning about.

And the more of it I dedicated to memory, the further from the real truth of things I seemed to drift. The only motivation that saw me through the endless mire of symbolic theory was to achieve worthy enough symbolic points in the scary mirage of final exams, so that I could go away and study more symbols where I wanted to after school ended, and hopefully, this would eventually provide the opportunity to finally earn some real experiences of my own.

School learning felt like lugging a wheelbarrow full of words around. The choice put forth was carrot or stick. And for the carrot, I lugged. I whistled along to a tune that wouldn't know itself unless it was written down.

But of course, symbols like these words you're reading now also have the power to guide us towards experiencing new inner light. Vast territories of one's own soul can be inspired to open up suddenly through the right key or symbol. Have you ever had that experience where you read something in a book for the first time, but you instantly know that you already knew it? That on some deep level, you had realised this thing before in some fashion, but it had remained shapeless in the dark of your subconscious? As a young'un, it was that feeling of connection to the world through words that lit me up like a firecracker more than anything else and made me ravenous for reading my own books.

Once, when I was a pimply little seventeen-year-old, I was sitting reading Richard Dawkins's *The God Delusion* in an empty train-station waiting room. In that book, there is a passage about sexual desire which goes like this: 'Sexual desire is sexual desire and its force, in an individual's psychology, is independent of the ultimate Darwinian pressure that drove it. It is a strong urge which exists independently of its ultimate rationale.'

It was such an immense thrill to read something that I already knew but hadn't realised – nor had I ever seen it expressed or written down – that I got a permanent marker out of my bag and wrote the entire quote out on the train station's waiting-room wall. Which took up a fair bit of wall. Years later, I went back to see if my odd vandalism still remained, but some misfortunate employee had scrubbed it off.

It's also interesting to look at the way in which the *story* of reality becomes encoded in us early on. Typically, in the form of the three-act story structure: the dilemma, the journey and the resolution. There is adversity of some kind in the dilemma, so the hero(es) must go on the journey to overcome it. And then, they overcome it in act three in the resolution, which typically signifies the 'end' of the story. All wrapped up neatly with a bow.

In school, the subject of history taught us about the past in this format: conflict/journey/resolution formatted chunks, like the French Revolution, or the Second World War, or the fight for Irish independence.

And all of our myths, popular movies, folk tales and advertising commercials tend to follow this same three-act structure, which states: 'Until such time as the dragon is slayed/castle is breached/ princess is rescued/I get that shaving foam/I gain or lose this many kilograms, I must defer a piece of happiness while striving for it.'

And in my business, a story doesn't even qualify as a story *until* you've come up with a good ending.

But could this way of learning about life early on, through symbols and three-act stories, have something to do with suffering?

Starting out in this book, I found myself in misery. Operating solely on the belief that, put simply: 'When I get what I want (success, blah-blah-blah), *then* I get the happiness. When my journey ends, by attaining *the resolution* of success, then it's happily ever after for me.'

Unknowingly, unconsciously, I was trying to jam a square peg into a round hole. I was trying to contrive life into a symbolic shape that aped this three-act story structure.

And it's interesting how, typically, it is often the instinct of the young, talented artist to put a bomb under the three-act story structure, by embracing other ways of storytelling, which could be defined specifically as not in the traditional three-act structure. They flirt with this for a while and call it surrealism or absurdism or punk, or whatever, and then eventually the majority return like salmon swimming back upstream towards the three-act blueprint, which provides the most comforting and familiar rhythm – not to mention the most financial stability.

This early programming, at this stage in our evolution, may pull the wool over our young eyes and prevent us from seeing the real truth: that there are no permanent resolutions. There are no such things as endings.

The human condition is a never-ending (until it ends) series of conflicts, journeys, resolutions, discoveries, dreams fulfilled, dreams abandoned, sunrises and sunsets.

And because this symbolic form of reality, through the three-act story programming, is ingrained in us from such a young age, I have a sneaking suspicion that it might be setting us up, not necessarily to fail, but setting us up with an unreasonable expectation of the future. And a lower opinion of the present.

Joe Frank, the great radio philosopher, mused that this is exactly why soap opera is the most accurate form of storytelling, because it most closely resembles the true nature of reality. Week in, week out, the characters become embroiled in new spicy dramas, find new solutions, which only turn back into more problems again.

And this is pertinent not only on an individual consciousness level, but also in our very systems of government. All ideologies that run countries find their bedrock in myth. A society must be, first and foremost, a triumphant story of unity, which binds all of its inhabitants together as one. The myth of the American Dream, for example, is a meritocratic myth because it is about the *pursuit* of happiness. Happiness is not inherent, it must be pursued and caught up with. Like a greyhound would a hare.

And one pursues happiness by working hard and making money.

Dilemma: I am poor.
Journey: I work hard enough to gain a good foothold in the marketplace.
Resolution: I am rich now. I am happy.
Story complete . . . ?

If I were to re-imagine the early education programming a little, I would add in one more key stage. So instead of the three-act story structure it would have a fourth and go: dilemma, journey, resolution, *repeat*. Which at the very least sets up a young mind with a more realistic idea of the future, and is less likely to lead them to feelings of dissatisfaction if they end up not achieving whatever it was they set themselves up to achieve.

The three-act story, as it is, subtly distracts from the true nature of the human condition. That happiness is not conditional on there being a pursuit, or a beginning, or an end to anything. Happiness comes through connection, to oneself and others, and creating things together, which creates a sense of community, a feeling that we are all part of something larger than ourselves. Then, one becomes aware on an experiential level that it is folly to defer one's happiness to some point further down the road, and instead finds it all right here and now.

This is what sticking with the practice of meditation made me more deeply, more experientially understand. That all of my conditioning from a young age that I experience to do with deferring my happiness to some point in the future, for example through anticipatory doubts, woes and anxieties about the future, are as fairy-tale as happily ever after.

Planning out my future is useful sometimes, but worrying about my future is to muddy the motion of my ever-present. And this, I believe, is the true dilemma of life. And it is a real Catch-22, because to chronically muddy one's ever-present with a worrisome future is the very thing that prevents happily ever after from having the chance to arrive.

Learning to break my three-act symbolic story conditioning, by embracing right now through melting into magnificent movingness, was to come to the realisation that when I trust in my present moment (because, after all, I am helplessly trapped in its eternal amber), the present moment provides. Which acts as a kind of roadmap for the playing out of our lives.

Then again, seeing as cultures all around the world keep telling their stories in the three-act dilemma/journey/resolution format, it becomes a question of chicken and egg. And prompts the enquiry: does the three-act story create our blueprint or does our blueprint create the three-act story?

And what if real, lasting happiness in life has less to do with the content of the stories we tell, and more to do with the structures of the stories we tell?

This feels a bit like Carrie from *Sex And the City*, signing off her column with some compelling questions for you the readers/viewers to dwell upon. In our household growing up, it was considered scandalous to speak out loud the title of that show. And when the *ohm*-like HBO sound came on the telly preceding it, I got a real Pavlovian pang of excitement in my (lower) belly.

How about first thing in the morning in school, once all the kids have shuffled into their first classes, still a bit tired and waking up, some heads are still on the schoolbus, they learn how worthwhile it is to integrate themselves in to the new present moment together for a minute or two at the start of class? Relax the vibration a little, shake off the interference of the recent past, focus the minds into one mind, and then boom, on with the show.

To marinate in meditation is to become more deeply enterained with that which cannot be named, that which sustains our lives – so where better to build those corridors of connection than in places of learning?

And again after big lunch, maybe. When the kids come bar-relling in chatting and still oscillating like they're on a basketball court. They sit down and tune back in by taking some nice con-scious breaths, maybe say a little thank-you for the feeling of aliveness, have a two-minute silent stillness session, and return as a group to a more coherent frequency?

These narrow nomindness corridors of time en masse would be a great little start in getting the most profit out of the practice for us all. It would be useful not least because it would help to restore attention spans. Several teaching practitioners have told me that in this incredibly stimulating screen age, they have found it more and more difficult to retain their student's focus for pro-longed periods of time.

And individually, it would lead to great expansions in intelli-gence. Just those few minutes a day would become important to some students, allowing them to discern a great deal of the fla-vours of their own consciousness, and catalyse many of them to continue on their own voyages at home.

Through his work, Beckett exposes the symbolic reality and everybody who mistakes it for the real thing.

By depicting 'no things', he is drawing into focus what is there in us in the absence of the activity of the critical, language-centric mind. The part of the mind that is forever grasping, asking, critiquing, seeking direction or pursuing a goal. Beckett was a Taoist. He was a Zen monk in a black polo neck.

Beyond the safe, yet sometimes stifling, symbolic world, his characters suffocate in broken symbols in the real world. Most of their dialogue is a purposeful affront to the rational thinking mind, the part of us tasked with decoding and making sense out of all the symbols. So anyone who came to see our *Endgame* and tried to watch it with their analytical mind switched on instead of their heart came away baffled and not very touched.

There was one night near the end of our run when, right at the very end of the play, as Hamm put his bloodied kerchief back over his dying face and the stage lights suddenly dropped, and we were all plunged into the darkness together, out of that charged silence, clear as day, I heard a lady halfway back in the audience hiss, 'Oh, thank fuck!'

Because Beckett had the instincts of Zen, he was naturally tuned to a deeper sense of what the Situationists innately felt – that reality is not fixed, it is a state of perpetual changefulness.

'We are born astride the grave.'

Samuel Beckett

From that perspective, considering the swiftness of revolutions of the revolving door of life and death, these symbols that we use during the life part of the turn seem almost provincial. And our desire to know things and translate them into opinions and beliefs is in itself a kind of clownish instinct. Like Clov, dangling desperately from the window ledge from one hand and reaching for the ladder with his other foot. The one thing that Clov, my character, clings to is order. And as such, when we first meet him, he goes huffing and puffing into an obsessive-compulsive Buster Keaton-style ritual of opening tiny windows up a dodgy ladder. His own little patch of order is in the kitchen (which the audience never gets to see) where he finds only a compensatory sliver of sanctuary in an otherwise chaotic world. Order is Clov's symbol of security. And the longer he clings on to it, the more it destroys his hopes of having any kind of a real life. And as the play rolls on, Clov must find it within himself to abandon the illusory safety of order in order to be saved.

Jesus Christ was credited with saying, 'Thou shalt not make to thyself any graven *image*, nor the likeness of anything that is in heaven above . . . Thou shalt not bow down to them, nor worship them.'

And Jesus's form, his body, had to be destroyed and reborn for him to become a true symbol of god. If his physical form had just ended, and not been dispatched and resurrected, endlessly, mirroring the appearance and disappearance of life, his story would not have accurately reflected the true nature of reality.

Beckett strips away belief and makes a clown out of believers, in order to talk about the nature of belief. He removes all love and compassion to create a conversation about love and compassion. He strips language down to its bare bones to nudge you towards seeing everything that is there in its absence.

> 'Every word is like an unnecessary stain on silence and nothingness.'
>
> Samuel Beckett

Ha! What a hoot. Despite it being a fun way to pass an afternoon, one need not heavy Beckett's *Endgame* with meanings at all because it only adds unnecessary layers. Just like the unfolding practice of embodying the inner light of life, *Endgame* is in/of/ about complete meaninglessness, which may sound bleak, but it isn't, it is the opposite. Meaninglessness is joy incarnate.

At exactly the halfway point of our show, there was this long pause which hung in the air directly after Nagg's curse, where he wishes a painful and lonely death on his son, Hamm, before disappearing back inside his bin.

And, egged on by our mischievous director, Danya, this halfway pause grew and grew in length into a kind of impromptu group meditation with the audience. Being energetically silent with that many people in a room was electrifying.

As the pause settled in, first it brought to the fore all the little shuffling sounds of the 371 bodies on their seats. The throat-clearings, and the hot stage lights clicking above my back felt like a metronome. Outside the theatre to the right could be heard the *dring-dring* of a passing streetcar, and a seagull intimidating another seagull over a scrap of Subway sandwich. In that long, delicious pause, I leapt at the opportunity to go into full marination mode. Bodyscanning down into the energy cascading up through the soles of my feet so as to allow gravity in to its fullest extent. Settling right down into Clov's crooked posture, and then dissolving my awareness in with the room's. And what sang by far the loudest, over all the noises, was the crackling energy of shared silence and nothingness.

It was Frankie who punctured it with, 'Our revels now are ended.' And on nights when the play asked for it, he stretched the pause out to easily a good minute and a half. Once afterwards, he told me how he had begun daydreaming inside the pause, sitting in his wheelchair behind his blacked-out goggles, and for a while forgot that he was doing a play or sitting in front of an audience at all.

It was priceless to be given such long spells of sacred silence with nearly 400 people. In that charged-up atmosphere, I found myself wishing it wouldn't end. And it gave me a curiosity to try to finagle more group meditation sessions.

To bring many souls together, who already have a seed of intuition growing, to know for ourselves the godpower we can generate, not in making any sound, but being in receipt of it.

Here's a useful little technique to try while practising meditation. I don't know what it's called but I call it labelling.

On my first silent retreat, we were taught the technique of mental labelling – where we notice the usual activity of random mental forms, but with the added step of *labelling* the themes of each one.

As thoughts and sensations whizz by, instead of paying them the energy of mind we slap a little Post-it note label on them to summarise each one thematically. And then let them off the hook and back into the ocean of subconscious out of which they were caught.

A little Post-it note label really helps to identify and define the theme of a mental form as it goes through awareness as something separate from pure awareness itself.

The names for my label themes arose quite organically. They included:

'Future': a conjuring of a perceived future. This is typically where I remind myself of that thing I still have to do.

'Desire to get up and do something': a sensation of restlessness in my body which doesn't necessarily have a visual component to it.

'Past ego': where I passively re-enact a scene from my past and sometimes even rewrite the story of it to make myself seem more successful/superior/dominant in it. This reflex, I believe, can be a source of a great deal of unnecessary suffering.

'Future ego': similarly, where I passively re-enact a scene in my perceived future, and make myself look superior/dominant in some way.

'The toad of possessiveness': this appeared in the form of a nauseating sensation in my gut, and as an image of a grumpy, warty-looking toad sitting in my actual gut. This one was caused by strong feelings of jealousy I was having during that retreat around the person I love.

It wasn't necessary to create that many labels. After just a short while, the themes of my monkey mind became very predictable.

So predictable, in fact, that it began to resemble a glitchy Windows 93. And the absurdity of it when held up to present scrutiny even began to make me laugh thinking, 'Who is this chattering lunatic at a bus stop who has had such influence over my life?'

Once I had identified and labelled the theme of a mental form, and it whizzed off into the beyond, the reinforcement of what remained, the pure awareness rich emptiness, that which defied labelling, was deeply, deeply potent.

Labelling and categorising the themes of my mind's involuntary activity brought a new kind of clarity, one I'd never felt before.

I cannot convey to you how exhilarating it was to apply this technique while lying in bed on night three of silent contemplation. After a few days without the distraction of screens, talking or delicious poisons, how quickly in stillness I reached a state of deep subconscious, which I call the field of infinite dreams – an incredibly vivid, holographic projection of subconscious hallucinations, the details of which defy language. We will come back to that a little later in the book.

Why not relax to the point of relaxation, then relax a little deeper, using the aforementioned techniques, and then give labelling a go? It's a useful tool when starting off on the journey because it has two useful applications:

1. It gives the inner focus something to 'do', the absence of which can cause discomfort at the beginning, before awareness is a little riper.
2. It reduces the significance and potency of mental/ emotional forms created by the reflex mind. It dethrones the mind, takes the spotlight off it, and instead shines it on what encloses the mind, what vastness sits there unchanging, staring us all in the face.

I have always been spidery about acting. A bit shy and solitary. I've done few classes, that type of thing. If ever there's a new character on my plate to explore, the first phases of exploration are done alone. Pacing around talking to the walls at home. Or pacing around talking to myself in the park.

What can really fray my nerves is the fact that, in solitude, by definition it is only possible to work on *half* of the character. Preparing for a performance in private that will be inevitably done in public is tantamount to prepping for a tennis match by banging a ball against a brick wall.

And oddly, in my business, it has been my experience that the *larger* the budget of the film or TV series, the *less* rehearsal of the material we do beforehand.

For some reason, rehearsal time is inversely proportionate to budget. I could draw a simple graph, where the horizontal axis would be labelled 'Rate of Rehearsal', and the vertical axis would be 'Budget'.

On bigger films and TV, typically you come in on day one, you're put into a trailer, you're ordered a coffee, and then summoned to a hair and makeup trailer where you might get lucky and bump into one of the other actors in passing that you're due to do the scene with that day.

An actor's art cannot be fully realised in solitude, and yet, most of the preparation on the biggest-budgeted films and TV I've worked on over the years was done in solitude. To me, this seems like a concerning oversight on such whopping investments.

And having prepared (mostly) in private self, when I step out onto the studio sound stage, now in public self, obviously, much of the discovery I have made at home or in my hotel room can and often does go out the window. I have been silently *grasping*, panicked: 'Oh god, I neither know nor feel anything about this character, and we're about to shoot the first scene. But last night, he felt so right there in the pocket!' Quite literally the stuff of nightmares. It's a strange feeling of coming to school with no homework done, even though you did your homework.

Context and environment has everything to do with the music that's being played on the actor's instrument (themselves). David Tennant once referred to the actor's terror as 'the dreaded curse'. But the nuances of acting need not be relegated to the shadowy back alleys of superstition. Acting is quantum!

In quantum physics, which is the study of how the most fundamental building blocks of reality behave, there exists a complicated phenomenon known as 'quantum superposition'. The important thing to know about quantum superposition is that it demonstrates two things. Firstly, that a subatomic particle, like the electron of an atom or a photon of light, just like the ones that make up our bodies and everything else, can exist in two forms or 'positions' at the same time. And secondly, subatomic particles behave differently depending on what they are interacting with.

The physicist Carlo Rovelli says: 'I think it is time to take [quantum] theory fully on board, for its nature to be discussed beyond the restricted circles of theoretical physicists and philosophers, to deposit its distilled honey, sweet and intoxicating, into the whole of contemporary culture.'

I couldn't agree more. Integrating what we now know about the wonderfully bizarre nature of reality would be a great help to those of us whose job it is to recreate reality. If I started an acting course tomorrow, two mandatory classes on every student's courseload would be morning meditation practice, and quantum mechanics.

Quantum anxiety (*idiom, informal*): Worrying in private about how you will do in public. In Irish English, comparable to the phrase 'shitting a large brick'.

My own personal definition. It is exciting to me how quantum physics offers language based in scientific research, not in superstition, to describe this peculiar adversity in acting.

This is also true for me personally, by the way, not just while I'm acting. Because for me, to truly like someone and get on with them, I must also *like myself* while in their company. To enjoy them, I must enjoy the reflection of myself being mirrored back at me.

My closest friends are the ones who are permissive enough to mirror back my most childish, idiotic, surreal self, and as reward for this they receive consistent levels of loving abuse. I silently

asphyxiate around those who try to drag me into a tone of practised earnestness.

Just like all my other misunderstood emotions, I always left
my quantum anxiety unaddressed. I rejected it as not real, and
avoided examining it closely, and as such for many years, the
'curse-breaking' part of a new job, the process of quantum-leaping
from the superposition of private self to public self, was a real
source of dread.

This is also the main reason why being an actor makes more
sense in the theatre. In preparation, all of the human doings
involved actually gather in a room together in advance. To laugh,
cry, debate, have a moan and wear the characters' shoes in each
other's company for weeks before performing the show.

Now, this actor's quantum anxiety is a tricky thing to mone-
tarily define in large-scale film and TV production. I think
probably one reason why rehearsal doesn't happen in big-budget
film and TV is because before my time, some clever producers
figured out that in-depth rehearsal means an in-depth investiga-
tion of what is in the script, which often results in the discovery of
mistakes or inconsistencies, which inevitably results in script
changes, and script changes result in more time and more money.
So instead, best just not. Best breed rehearsal out of the culture of
large scale film- and TV-making altogether. Save money upfront
and blindly hope for the best.

But imagine, on average, how much better told our stories
would be if the 'curse' of the actor's quantum anxiety was more
widely understood and catered for. How much more emotional
range would be earned to enrich a story in advance of telling it if
the big producers of films and television – studios, networks and
streaming platforms – understood the financial and qualitative
value of rehearsal? How much more acting talent would emerge?

On *Misfits*, a not-very-high-budget UK TV series, we the five main delinquents were *drilled* for two weeks in a rehearsal room before filming anything. And by the end of that we were thick as thieves.

I remember clowning around a lot and our director, Tom, stopping me for a second:

'Listen, Nathan is a real person. He's not just an onstage act. This shit is really happening to him. Play it real, play the reality of it. It's always funnier that way.'

Once, the producers even tricked us into going on a military obstacle course. The five of us donned our trademark boiler suits for the first time, but these were military-green ones, and we were slung headfirst into a gruelling afternoon of rope-climbing, under-barb-wire crawling and wading through giant tracts of mud with the drill instructor fellow in camo pants and little pointy hat shouting at us from the sides. We banded together like soldiers in a war on that obstacle course, and no (wo)man was left behind. And at the end, we all staggered across the finish line arm-in-arm, drenched in mud, sweat and tears.

As a result of all this, what landed on screen later was something more lived in, more natural and from the heart, because it wasn't encumbered by inhibitive quantum anxiety, by none of the natural guardedness people carry in their bodies after having just met. My acting career owes a lot to those two weeks of rehearsal and that obstacle course. It was the difference between us *Misfits* riding a five-person tandem bicycle and wobbling all over the road, and riding a five-person tandem bicycle smoothly and confidently.

Henry Gustav Molaison was a young man who suffered from debilitating seizures, which worsened into his early adult years.

Eventually, in 1953, he underwent a radical surgery to remove parts of his brain known as the hippocampus, the area believed to be causing his seizures.

Unwittingly, they turned him into a 'pure amnesiac', meaning none of his other faculties were remotely affected, only his memory. After surgery, he was in fine health, but could not remember much of the eleven years before.

The breakthrough here was the discovery that, although Molaison could no longer call to mind memories of his life, he could still carry out things like writing or riding a bicycle. And he could even learn how to do new things if they were practised over and over.

It was this case that gave us insight into the fact that we human doings possess two ways of storing long-term memory.

'Implicit memory and explicit memory are both types of long-term memory. Information that you remember unconsciously and effortlessly is known as implicit memory, while information that you have to consciously work to remember is known as explicit memory. Knowing how to ride a bike or read a book relies on implicit memory. Consciously recalling items on your to-do list involves the use of explicit memory.'

Kendra Cherry, Verywellmind.com

From a neuroscientific standpoint, this is what the importance of rehearsal is all about. Would you rather be watching actors in a film who are drawing their characters from their 'to-do list' memories, or effortlessly from their implicit memories? If you are a financier, the Big Cheese, wouldn't you rather pay for a movie – a movie that will likely cost you millions and many years of your life from inception to release – with souls on screen who are embodying the story, not trying to recall it?

That's why nowadays, I take a new character for long walks. I ask him questions all about his life: 'What were you doing before this story kicks off? What are your plans after? What's your favourite building on this street?'

And after a certain amount of hours on our walk, of him auto-rambling answers to all my enquiries, and me pretending to be him to unknowing shopkeepers, he eventually gets promoted from my explicit memory up into my implicit memory. Meaning, now I can access him without having to recall him to mind.

So, if you do ever see me wandering around in circles and talking to myself in the park, best leave me be because my character might be dangerous and lash out.

Actors are of importance to us all, you know. They can make or break a story. A good performance can make us fall in love. It can take us on a journey through the actor's dimension, which makes us question the way we take for granted how we relate to each other and ourselves emotionally.

They can subvert presupposed notions of what it means to be a human doing, and as such, shed light on new space to move into. How many countless individuals have been compelled to model their identities after an acting performance that touched them? How many quiffs did James Dean inspire? How many blondes did Marilyn Monroe? How many real-world fight clubs did people get into because of *Fight Club*?

There is great value in applying what we now know about the quantum mirage of reality to the language of acting: the job of recreating the mirage.

Of our physical world, Max Planck, one of the fathers of quantum physics, who rewrote the laws of thermodynamics said:

> As a man who has devoted his whole life to the most clearheaded science, to the study of matter, I can tell you as a result of my research about the atoms this much: There is no matter as such! All matter originates and exists only by virtue of a force which brings the particles of an atom to vibration and holds this most minute solar system of the atom together ... We must assume behind this force the existence of a conscious and intelligent Mind. This Mind is the matrix of all matter.

He observed down at the Planck scale, down in the subatomic solar systems of atoms, that reality appears and disappears on and off like a movie projector. Flashing a kind of complex 'image' on and off, on and off, action and rest, at an incredibly fast rate. At room temperature, an atom oscillates between these two states like a pendulum at about 10^{15} (or 1 quadrillion) times per second.

In the school of Tibetan Buddhism, they arrived at an eerily similar deduction:

'The tangible world is movement, say the Masters, not a collection of moving objects, but movement itself. There are no objects 'in movements', it is the movement which constitutes the objects which appear to us: they are nothing but movement. This movement is a continued and infinitely rapid succession of flashes of energy (in Tibetan *tsal* or *shoug*). All objects perceptible to our senses, all phenomena of whatever kind and whatever aspect they may assume, are constituted by a rapid succession of instantaneous events.'

Alexandra David-Neel and Lama Yongden,
The Secret Oral Teachings in Tibetan Buddhist Sects

I find it thrilling how quantum physics and ancient Tibetan Buddhism overlap by arriving at basically the same conclusion concerning the nature of our reality.

Through practising stillfulness, embodying rest to witness all the action, the oscillation of one's atoms change down to a measurably slower frequency, or rate of 'on/offs' per second. And, deeply enough down, the movement of a marinating human doing begins to resonate at the same frequency as planet Earth. And not just planet Earth, but our whole entire cosmos.

Itzhak Bentov is another fascinating character, because he was both a genius inventor and a genius meditator. He applied his scientific mind to the measuring of consciousness, and applied his ability to practise embodying deep consciousness to science. Through his work, he embodied the compelling overlap between the scientific and the mystic view of things.

'We may say now that in deep meditation the human being and the planet system start resonating and transferring energy. This is occurring at a very long wavelength of about 40,000km, or just about the perimeter of the planet. In other words, the signal from the movement of our bodies will travel around the world in about one-seventh of a second through the electrostatic field in which we are embedded. Such a long wavelength knows no obstacles, and its strength does not attenuate much over large distances. Naturally, it will go through just about anything: metal, concrete, water, and the fields making up our bodies. It is the ideal medium for conveying a telepathic signal.'

Itzhak Bentov, *Stalking the Wild Pendulum:*
On the Mechanics of Consciousness

This feels like the right moment to go back and revisit in greater detail what I call the field of infinite dreams.

When a long enough frequency of consciousness is being emitted in restfulness, one can encounter the field of infinite dreams.

Where the light that I can detect in my awareness with my eyes closed goes from incoherent, meaning all fuzzy and blurry, to coherent, where it begins to form vivid pictures and scenes. Tapestries of psychotropic dreams flit payfully across the landscape of my inner sight with incredible clarity, like the murmurations of a flock of birds, in such a way as to defy all surface language. Other than to broadly say it's (kind of) like dreaming only you're wide awake.

But more specifically, like lucid dreaming while you're wide awake, because in a lucid dream a person is dreaming while also being aware that they are dreaming. To be in the field of infinite dreams is not like thinking, either passively or actively so. With passive thinking, one can get carried away from present awareness on the saddle of a bolting thought. And with active thinking, one sets the mind to working out a problem, encouraging the imagination to flex its muscles. So active thinking is effectively using the mind, *wielding* the mind in service of drawing that picture or fixing that leak or whatever, whereas in the field of infinite dreams, no mind use is necessary whatsoever.

In the field, you are in receipt of the stuff that thoughts are made of – the inner light – arranging itself into complex holographic forms, rearing up and splashing back down like the surface of a playful ocean, but all the while you are remaining very much in the present as the Watcher.

If our existence's basis is movement, then it means that reality exists along a kind of movement spectrum, which runs the gamut between extreme movement and absolute rest. Through stillness, we are exploring along this spectrum, by moving our rate of consciousness from typical movement, 10^{15} on/offs per second, towards stillness. Stillness, a whole other face on the coin of our consciousness.

We are all of us a cosmos of mini solar systems called atoms, the nuclei of which are the suns, who are given our perception by virtue of vibrating light and matter by virtue of vibrating electrons.

To really begin to internalise this is to stop identifying solely with the feeling of the bodymind, and to also begin identifying with the space around/inside the feeling of the body.

It is to see that the information that you are perceiving, reciprocating, noticing, not noticing, is all constituted by the AM/FM radio frequency along which your consciousness is currently surfing. Practising beingness by itself over time very gently twists the knob on the dial around to broaden one's bandwidth, so as to enjoy premium access to a wider range of stations that reality has to offer.

We have seen how it is in our very nature to exist in (at least) two places at the same time, both as separate and as one. We are a quantum superposition.

And every single individual has the same intrinsic value here, because, irrespective of what stage of consciousness they are at, when it comes to practising spacefulness, one is expanding their own personal limits.

The Dream

As time rolled on, things began to evolve naturally from stillness just sitting still, to practising stillness while on the move.

The author Rebecca Solnit called walking, 'A state in which the mind, the body, and the world are aligned'. Which, as it goes, would also serve as a pretty accurate description for meditation. Usually when you hear a talented athlete or musician or whoever describing how it feels to be immersed in their zone, the description serves perfectly as a description for a nice practised sit in sublime spaciousness. Clarity of mind, characterised by no thought, with mind and body acting as one peacefully, not pitted against one another.

Friedrich Nietzsche wrote: 'What my foot demands in the first place from music is that ecstasy which lies in good walking.'

I was out on a long walk home through a wintry Toronto. The ice was crunching under my boots, and my groceries were all in one big bag, the handle of which was digging something ferocious into my collarbone.

Rolling past the Rolling Stones bar on Queen Street, clarity left me and a self-awareness kicked in. Which made me retroactively notice the prolonged gap of time before that which had gone by with no thinking. I wanted to return there, to the thought-less realm, so as I walked, I began rhythmically *ohm mahne padme hum*-ing.

Inwardly repeating the mantra *ohm mahne padme hum*, to the bouncing rhythm of my footsteps. Two steps *ohm*, two steps *mahne*, two steps *padme*, and the last *hum* steps varied. Swinging to the beat of the syllables if I found the moment (re)blurred by a flurry of thoughts. And in this way, walking became music.

In the prolonged cessation of mind this *ohm*-walking caused, I got to simply enjoy the tapestry of the world unfurling without the unneeded inner commentary/judgement. Which included a gregarious middle-aged woman walking up to two other women at the intersection, one of whom was in a wheelchair. She slapped her gloved hands together and then threw her arms warmly out and proclaimed, 'Good afternoon, ladies!', and just as she bent over to greet the lady in the chair, she snuck $15 into her hand, but discreetly, so the other lady wouldn't see. I saw on my side as I *ohm*-ed by.

Then, a brown-eyed kid on a bicycle came racing up and shouted precociously at his little brother, also on a bike, 'Hey, remember that time you spoke four seconds ago?'

Just then, a man came screeching up onto the pavement in his car like a cop in *The Blues Brothers*, leapt out, and sprinted through a nearby open doorway. And he had barely run in before barrelling back out with a large brown bag (of food, presumably), car door slamming and screeching away again.

Ohm, two, three, four . . .

Then, my attention was taken away up into the sky by two enormous, swirling, jostling murmurations of pigeons sweeping by over the dollar store. Flirting against the backdrop of an orange evening, like wind made of birds. And they made me wonder, 'Who orchestrates this big group move? How are they exchanging enough information to fly so closely together in beautiful synchronicity without bumping into each other?' Indication of consciousness operating as a collective mind there, in my view. One shared mind among individuals, like a shoal of feathery sky fish.

(Barely) *Ohm mahne padme . . .*

I stopped at the entrance of a small mosque, next to an ornate Gothic-looking door which, ironically, on closer inspection, was the door to a small, quite plain real estate office. Two men stood studying the mosque's notice board closely.

It was about Covid closures. When I stopped and read what they were reading, one of the men turned and looked at me over his blue face mask, but with welcome as if to say, 'Hello. You are curious.' His eyes were big and beautiful and serious and large and light brown.

As I turned off Queen Street, *ohm*-ing away, I saw a sad, faded pink heart that had been painted on the top floor of a house about five houses down. I'd walked past that house innumerable times and never noticed the faded pink heart. On the house's front stoop, a man wearing a hat with earflaps was serenading a woman in the front yard, singing into the blade end of a shovel: 'When I get that feelin', I want sexual healin'.'

I diverted off Queen Street for the purposes of strolling onto her quieter parallel counterpart, Anti-Queen Street, as I call it. Toronto natives surely know Queen Street, but running parallel along most of her right side east to west are stretches of back alleyways which have no names. They are very interesting, because instead of walking along Queen with the din of its traffic and the visual roar of the marketplace, Anti-Queen in parallel is quiet, and decorated with the most beautiful art. The only sounds are

the air conditioners rumbling in summer. And there are giant sur-
realist murals and grand sweeping colourful portraits. Toronto has
lots of these nameless, quiet little alleyways, and it's some of the
best walking in the city.

So there was I, strolling absorbently, and suddenly considered this: in the stillness and quiet, one can't help noticing how
all human perception is layered. We experience reality from the
inside out as a kind of onion of sensations that go in this order:
sensation of body, sensation of mind's activity, the sum of the
external world.

Typically, on a walk, as I bowl along, it feels normal to be
passively commenting on/judging the world as I pass through it,
but the *ohm*-walking drum took this reflex out of the equation.
And reminded me that the world is an open case file until it's
judged shut. To *not* judge the world is to become the world, and
to get to experience the onion-y sensation of both the external
stimuli and their correlating inner responses, while remaining
coolly aware of both.

Lao Tzu, after he'd wiped, polished and pulled up his pants
and was on his way back to his cabin, thought to jot this down:

> Watch your thoughts, they become your words; watch
> your words, they become your actions; watch your
> actions, they become your habits; watch your habits,
> they become your character; watch your character, it
> becomes your destiny.

Watching the sensations of my mind on my walk, while not taking
them very seriously, meant having the awareness to ask not
whether my judgements were right, but what their appearances
were indicative of.

I used to carry a false notion of how being a person worked. I relied on my mindstream reflexively to tell me what I thought. I gave thinking overall too much weight, and as a result, thoughts were heavier loads to carry.

On this stroll I toyed around with the *ohm*-walk some more. Prolonging the recitation of each mantra sound way out into a drone over the rhythm of many steps, or speaking the mantra downwards through my spine like light, or catapulting it out of my body and down into the earth below the pavement, or sending it flying like fireworks out the top of my head. And after a short time of this I went into a deep trance, and the *ohm* sound evolved indescribably. It deepened and settled in to become like a gentle inner drum, like my heart lightly playing a bongo, but a beat I no longer had to pay any attention to. The drum replaced my mind's activity layer of sensation almost altogether. It fell naturally into the position of where thinking used to be.

Da-dum, two, three, four, *ohm*, two, three, four, *mahne*, four, five, *padme*, six, seven, *hummmm* . . .

There were still stray cloudbursts of thought occasionally, but they were smaller and possessed considerably less ability to drag me into them. So instead, they were paid no mind as I bounced along to the beat of the drum.

I was Toronto forest bathing. Toronto is a machine forest, of sorts.

Shinrin-yoku, which translates from Japanese as 'forest bathing', is a term brilliantly dreamed up by the Japanese Ministry of Forestry and Other Stuff in the early 1980s to improve the overall health of their people by encouraging them to go for long strolls in the forest.

Akasawa Forest became Japan's first designated forest-bathing destination in 1982. They laid many kilometres of paths through it, over mountain streams, between giant cypress trees, and in late spring, flowers bloom on the forest floor which are said to look like stars scattered under your feet.

'Forests are an amazing resource. They give us everything we rely on in order to exist. They produce oxygen, cleanse the air we breathe and purify our water ... In addition to this, forests have always helped us to heal our wounds and to cure our diseases. And, from time immemorial, they have relieved us of our worries, eased our troubled minds, restored and refreshed us.'

Dr Qing Li, *Forest Bathing: How Trees Can Help You Find Health and Happiness*

Li was an instrumental figure in translating the innately positive feelings felt by forest bathing into the language of hard science. Forest bathing is a silent walking meditation, with no destination, in the nourishing company of our symbiotic pals, the trees. We softly return our attention back to the sense perceptions. The woody smell of phytoncides – organic aerosol compounds that trees emit as defence mechanisms against animals, which possess potent medicinal qualities if you're human – the gossiping of birds, the rustling of leaves, the crunch of detritus underfoot and the infinity of fractal expressions in nature all around.

Simply remaining with/in the sensual portals boosts our immune levels. It boosts the quantity and activity of NK (natural killer) cells in our bodies. Our sensual portals are like hospitals.

'Wherever there are trees, we are happier and healthier.'

Dr Qing Li

My little *ohm*-walking drum permitted me to allow the world to return to how it is when my sense of myself is not there. Which was not only pleasurable to be (in), but I had this knowing that by remaining in its absorbent, non-judgemental space, I was naturally deepening my power to exchange greater amounts of energy with it.

Giving the world a little rhythm, instead of constantly giving it what I thought about it, transformed it into a big savings account that declared 'Pay into me! The more you lodge, the more our bond matures.'

If I was attempting to be a waffly spiritual type (Me? Surely not . . .), then I would be inclined to call the *ohm*-walk technique, or moving meditation, a doorway to enlightenment.

I don't subscribe to the idea that this enlightenment business is a thing that only a handful of us in history have got to experience. Pah! Nonsense. Every soul on Earth has access.

I'd love to see *ohm*-walks becoming a thing, like the Situationists' *dérives* around Paris. Maybe this book will be their catalyst. I dream of groups of us coming together in shared walking, with no objective other than to listen to the music of the world.

Ohm-walks could be a new trend. Let's start making Instagram reels and TikTok videos. Then, once the *ohm*-walk becomes a viral sensation, *ohm*-walk group's tastes will start to atomise and become more refined. People of similar heights will begin banding together in *ohm*-walking clubs, so that it's easier for all to remain entrained in the same step. On one side of the park you'll see a very tall group all drifting like river reeds, and on the other side a group of little folk, all marching on the spot together with their eyes closed. Then, the two groups will square off and have a big medieval fight to the death. Or a big medieval cuddle. And then, one *ohm*-walking group will walk for hundreds of miles in attempts to secure the record for longest *ohm*-walk. Which will give rise to the *Ohm*-Walk Contemplation Championships where contestant groups set the routes of their own race and at the end, everyone wins.

But I wonder, would the *ohm*-walk require a little social courage? By courage, I mean getting beyond that awkward feeling of doing something together with other people you don't know very well while not speaking at all. But oh, the joy of being with other people and not feeling compelled to speak! The ease of spending time in other people's energy rather than in their company.

Also, a little courage to get beyond looking strange in public, perhaps? Drawing stares from strangers for looking 'weird' is some folks' worst nightmare.

Courage may well be what's required.

To make a leap of faith to embrace the quiet below all the incessant instruction of ego noise.

Hui-neng, the last patriarch of Zen who died in 713 AD, once shouted this off a rooftop before swan diving into the monastery's swimming pool:

Instead of *trying to purify* or empty the mind, one must simply let go of the mind – because the mind is nothing to be grasped. Letting go of the mind is also equivalent to letting go of the series of thoughts and impressions which come and go 'in' the mind, neither repressing them, holding them, nor interfering with them.

Let's give the dignity of Zen back to our public spaces. They have become dominated by mass transit and the marketplace. Groups of us coming together to embody what surrounds us, and help recalibrate the collective mind to where it's minding us a little less.

The world is so beautiful all by itself.

With the *ohm* sequencer going, I couldn't help noticing how all of me was still there after the thinking element of the mind had been let go. My sense of balance remained fully operational, my ability to identify a bus coming up the street and not get hit by it was all functioning famously. In fact, strolling in the present, undistracted by the past or the future, I felt far more there when thinking had gone away.

I didn't forget who I was and become a nihilist and suddenly not care about life. My connection to life increased, and so my love for it increased too. To bathe in the feeling of beingness is not a loss of self, it is the reclamation of self. And the integration of self with other. Being passionate about beingness by itself, and being passionate about other things are not mutually exclusive.

And even if I had the power to make my self-awareness completely disappear (which I don't), I would not want it to. Meditation makes me so happy because it is about accepting every part of my life 100 per cent. Making enemies with myself – any aspect, be it *ceantar* or *alltar* – would be a pointless waste of time.

And I happen to like that external me guy. The fellow who pops out when I have stuff to say to other people. He is very important to me; I need him to do my job and earn a living. And on rare occasions, he can be quite original.

Which brings me on to the whole reason why I began writing about this walk in the first place.

The *ohm*-walk inspired in me a two-pronged mission.

1. To be an advocate of the notion that we *do not even need a forest to forest bathe.*

    I believe that applying the simple techniques of forest bathing – tuning in to the sounds, the sights, smells and feels, marinating in our delicious sensory portals – is good for our health *anywhere.*

2. To extend the forests of the world beyond the borders of the forests.

    It is time to take what has now been proven about the substantial health benefits of forest bathing, and play with the idea of applying it to the rest of the world.

Let's start with point one. Not everybody has access to a forest. Now, strictly speaking, I don't know if we could still call this forest bathing; we can call it *ohm*-walking or 'city bathing', but for those of us who don't live near forests, we now have lots of scientific research to show that the practice of witnessing one's lifeforce both inside and out results in significant health benefits – greater rest and recovery, a decrease of bodywide inflammation, increase in immune system function, greater clarity of mind. And, although the health benefits may not be as substantial as the benefits of practising meditation while sitting or walking in a forest, there are real health benefits nonetheless. Forest bathing is simply bathing, but just in the context of a forest.

Now, I have found that when it comes to tuning in to my environment in the city, no matter where I am, using Alan Watts's meditative listening technique as the first step is most effective. Have you tried that one yet? Where you relax and accept all of the city's sounds around you as one big happening of sound. I find this works better with my eyes closed, because it's easier for the whole sonic landscape to create a kind of 'halo' or 'aura' of energy around me. Sound swaddles me in its blanket, and then all noises cease to be alarming, disturbing or distressing, and instead become *nourishing*.

In this very absorbent and accepting state, I am convinced that the sound of passing traffic can help to reduce inflammation in the body, that the sound of an ambulance siren can reduce anxiety, the sound of a train's wheels grinding against the tracks as it traverses a bend can lower blood pressure. (The only sounds I have discovered that can sabotage this for me are loud human voices.)

There no longer needs to be the hard-lined distinction of forest = good health, city = bad health.

When we relate to it softly and absorbently, sound becomes medicinal. Undoubtedly, the sounds of nature are still better for our health than the sounds of public transport, but they are still sounds nonetheless. And our sensual portals have been proven to act like little hospitals. The sounds of a city are rich, they arrive in awareness in all manner of interesting harmonies and frequencies. And the trick is not to identify them, but instead to let them pour into you like water.

Of *Pale Blue Dot*, the photograph of the Earth taken from six billion kilometres away in 1990, the American astronomer Carl Sagan said:

> Every hunter and forager, every hero and coward, every creator and destroyer of civilization, every king and peasant, every young couple in love, every mother and father, hopeful child, inventor and explorer, every teacher of morals, every corrupt politician, every 'superstar', every 'supreme leader', every saint and sinner in the history of our species lived there. On a mote of dust suspended on a sunbeam.

My pal Shane taught me a fascinating thing. We were talking about practising quietness, and he said no matter where we are, be it on a noisy train, or at home twiddling our thumbs, or orbiting the mosh pit of a death metal gig, we have the ability to tune in to the endless soundlessness of outer space. Out there in the blackness around our tiny dust mote is an endless abyss where sound cannot go. Beyond the hubbub of our village exists an expanse of silence which, if you try, you'll notice you can perceive.

It's there in the background, between the sounds, behind the sounds, like a familiar radio frequency, silently dwarfing all the other ones. And to listen for it is to become space itself, and envision our Earth from far away, being invisibly cradled in god's giant black cupped hand. And to hear it is to discover that your perception actually stretches far beyond even the confines of this planet. And if you've been marinating in meditation along with me, you'll notice that the silence you can hear up there in space is the exact same quality of silence that can be heard deep inside yourself.

I invented a new word: *fauln*. Which means listening to the world, including its activity inside your body, and inadvertently hearing two (or more) sounds occurring simultaneously that you've never noticed together before, and surprisingly, they complement each other beautifully.

I invented this word in the middle of a light and sparkly meditation session, between an *Endgame* Saturday matinee and the evening show, while sitting in the green room of the Gate Theatre in Dublin. Through the wall into the dressing rooms, I could hear the buzzing of an electric shaver, and then, out the open sash window, a double-decker Dublin bus trundled down the Rotunda towards O'Connell Street, and splashed through big puddles of rain. This *fauln* made me laugh out loud it felt so nice. Afterwards, I felt energised and refreshed, and ready for another evening of existential clowning.

Our inner/outer focus, when it learns to rest on a fixed point as opposed to darting around every few seconds, is doctoral. And when that settled focus is allowed to dissolve into our external reality through our senses, it sets the scene for homeostasis, meaning when the body tends towards balance and equilibrium. We might have been encouraged to forget all about this great power of ours through the endless avalanche of marketeering by the medical industries, that with just relaxation, patience and acceptance, we have the ability to heal ourselves with great potential.

Paracelsus, a sixteenth-century Swiss physician, philosopher and all-round great guy, who is also credited as the father of the early modern medical movement, said: 'The art of healing comes from nature, not from the physician.'

Another more recent all-round great guy was Akira Miyawaki, who pioneered the method of fast-growing mini-forests. His fast-growing mini-forests typically grow ten times faster and are a hundred times more biodiverse than forests planted by conventional means. And instead of taking the usual 200–300 years to grow, Miyawaki's take just twenty to thirty. In the documentary *Call of the Forest: The Forgotten Wisdom of Trees*, Miyawaki remarks how one really only needs 'eighteen square inches' to create a mini-forest, just like he did at the behest of the Ministry of Forests and Other Stuff's request across many cities in Japan.

I discovered Miyawaki's breakthrough through a company called *Afforestt*. Its founder, Shubhendu Sharma, was an engineer working in a Toyota car-manufacturing plant in India when he met Miyawaki, who had been given the task of fast-growing a forest to make Toyota's whole industrial operation carbon-neutral. Sharma was so fascinated watching this process that first he volunteered with Miyawaki, then he quit his job. And now:

'His company Afforestt promotes a standardized method for seeding dense, fast-growing, native forests in barren lands, using his car-manufacturing acumen to create a system allowing a multilayer forest of 300 trees to grow on an area as small as the parking spaces of six cars.'

TED.com

Sharma took the Miyawaki method, applied his own engineering wisdom, and further streamlined the miracle of fast-growing forests. Then, he shared his findings with the whole world via open-sourcing.

Which leads me back to what I was daydreaming about the other night: I want to build my own forest.

It will be a small but thriving tree metropolis with no name. It will have a tall wooden tower at its centre for looking out over the canopy as it grows. And it will have little clearings to make room for interesting artworks, and walkways where the branches embrace to make archways overhead.

I dream of sitting in my forest deep in meditation. It's dusk, and the trees around are emitting their healing chemistry, and the micro-rustles from the leaves and the little animals hunting and burrowing are making healing sounds.

I remember, just before the global lockdown in 2020, hearing reports of London's alarming rates of early-onset strokes affecting children as young as twelve years old, particularly in east London near where I lived. And it has been proven now that a major contributing factor to strokes is air pollution. Roughly fifteen million of us suffer strokes around the world every year, and about six million of us die from them.

Dr Vladimir Hachinski, co-founder of the World Brain Alliance, a fellowship of doctors who pool knowledge from their respective fields to tackle the growing issue of strokes, wrote: 'The most alarming finding [in a global survey conducted by the National Institute for Stroke and Applied Neurosciences at Auckland University of Technology] was that about a third of the burden of stroke is attributable to air pollution.'

And according to the Irish National Audit of Stroke (INAS) National Report 2020, stroke is the third leading cause of death in Ireland.

BMC Public Health, a peer-reviewed open-access journal which published a huge study in 2010 entitled 'The Incidence of

All Stroke and Stroke Subtype in the UK, 1985–2008' found that 'stroke also imposes an economic burden to the UK, costing about £7 billion a year, of which £2.8 billion are direct costs to the NHS.'

Notwithstanding the proven benefits to respiratory function, blood pressure, inflammation and overall mental wellbeing, but based on these concerning statistics, what we also stand to save by re-establishing more forestry and biodiversity includes brain damage.

Which brings us on to point two: extending the forests beyond the forests' borders. Just like the little corridors of quiet contemplation in the classrooms, we should weave lots of small corridors of fast-growing mini-forests through our cities, so that we can be more directly among the trees and their health benefits without having to go out of our way.

Instead of funnelling all of our health budget into the hospitals, why not play with turning the city into one big green hospital?

It would be so much nicer to be there, in the city, not least because it would take the edge off what botanist Diana Beresford-Kroeger calls 'the concrete experience'.

Here is another useful thing to try while exploring yourself in nameless consciousness. Practising becoming attuned to the river of shakti energy which flows within makes it possible to bathe the brain in bloodflow. A deep state of meditation gives us the means to give our brains a thorough massage without ever moving our hands. Where our focus goes, blood flows.

And after all, the brain is the big jelly in our heads responsible for our ability to speak, judge, foresee, associate with our external environments, imagine and remember. It governs emotional function, intellectual function, coordination, speech comprehension, seeing, hearing, smelling, physical sensation, voluntary movement, involuntary movement, swallowing and breathing, so it's worthwhile to give it a wee gander.

Sit up or lie down, embrace your true sight by closing your eyes. With a big, deep, relaxing breath, gently bring the laser pen of focus into your brain. Feel the fizz of energy rushing up your neck and downwards through the top of your head, and feel your brow softening fully on your exhale.

Let the spotlight of awareness move slowly around inside your skull, not forcing anything. From the front near your face, and right to the back, and all around the edges. Visualise a spectacular fireworks display igniting and illuminating the entire inside of your head with sparkling bright lights, which then fall slowly and blanket your entire brain in tingly awareness. Let light swirl around inside your head like a vortex. Play around with what energy you can manipulate at will inside your skull. Slowly but surely, and only if it doesn't feel forced, begin allowing the inner light to flow more quickly into your head.

Notice which areas inside are easier to feel, and the areas that are more elusive. Which parts feel 'lighter' and which feel 'darker'.

For me, the general left side of my brain feels darker than my right. It has always been this way since I first noticed it. So, I tend to gently direct the light of my focus towards there, bit by bit, and fill my brain up with light as best I can. I remember one of the first times I tried this sitting on my bed. After a short while of bathing my brain, I was visited by the most vivid memories of childhood that I hadn't thought of in years. They came crashing into my awareness like a ton of bricks, and they were so vivid I could quite literally feel the texture of the blue shorts I was wearing on my little ten-year-old legs.

Why not take ten or fifteen minutes, sit your ground, and give it a go?

I come from a town called Portlaoise.

It's a charming, infrastructural place nestled in Ireland's fertile belly, with plenty of civil services and plenty of farming.

The council recently announced an inspiring plan called '2040 and Beyond: A Vision for Portlaoise', which outlines ambitions for, among other things, '. . . the "greening" of the town centre to improve the environment and aid in promoting health and well-being of residents and visitors'.

To that bullet point of the strategy, I have an idea to add.

Portlaoise becomes the first town to create and install a groundbreaking town-wide carbon capture template, which becomes open-source for all other towns/cities around the world to try, by means of an exciting new competition called The Green Town Awards.

Think the Tidy Towns Awards but it's more geared towards replanting for the purposes of our egalitarian health, and less geared towards satisfying one's control impulses (no offense). In fairness though, the Tidy Towns Awards do include in their criteria 'Nature and Biodiversity in your Locality' for a possible 50 maximum points, in an overall marking out of 470 points. For 'Tidiness and Litter Control' you can win a possible 90 points.

Think of it through Shubhendu Sharma's evolution of Miyawaki's fast-growing forest method. Every little patch, every verge, every roadside wasteground now has the potential to become a forest that will flourish in biodiversity in twenty years.

Portlaoise becomes the first town to really extend the forest beyond the forest's borders. The Green Town Awards template will be such a success that it will catch fire (ha) and go global, and Portlaoise becomes an inspiring symbol in the great climate transition. The mayor of Portlaoise will be invited to all the summits and be given free tea and sandwiches.

The Green Towns would be awarded thusly:

☆ Best Lawn Replacement
☆ Best Street
☆ Best Use of Unused Residential Surface Area
☆ Best Use of Unused Commerical Surface Area
☆ Best Wildflower Patches
☆ Best Hedgerows
☆ Best Community Greening Education Project
☆ Best Use of Renewable Power
☆ Most Innovative Green Town Idea

And, the most jealously coveted:

☆ Greenest Town of All Award

The criteria by which towns would be nominated and selected for awards would be:

1. Quantity of Greenified Public Space – 100 points
2. Variety and Biodiversity of Native Species – 100 points
3. Beauty, Oh! Beauty – 100 points

Other than the pride of winning, the triumphant town committee would get to ride down the main street of Portlaoise in an old wooden carriage drawn by an electric SUV, hanging out the windows, sipping champagne and waving while people lob flowers and cash at them.

How to make the dream come true:

1.   Government-subsidised tree-planting schemes.
     Now that a town council can comfortably rely on a windfall of verifiable scientific research that proves that re-establishing a forest population will save them considerable money on the cost of health.
2.   Annual property tax and corporation tax incentives for individuals or companies who can provide evidence of a certain 'green growth' or 'green quota' per square metre. These metres may be horizontal or vertical.

We study old maps in the councils' public records to find the areas where trees once grew but have been cut down for one reason or another, and see about re-planting them. If they grew there once, they'll grow again.

And with the miracle of GPS (global positioning systems), the technology that the map on your phone is using, it's possible to map out the plantlife of any townland, who then might aim to accumulatively increase the quantity of that plantlife by, say, 25 per cent. You would only qualify for the *heats* of the Green Town Awards by showing at least a 10 per cent increase.

Thomas Crowther, of the Yale Climate and Energy Institute, did this in 2015. He conducted a global project counting trees with satellite imaging technology, and made a pretty educated guess that there were about 3.04 trillion trees on the planet. He also estimated that before the explosion of human civilisation, there were about 5.6 trillion trees. In just a few short centuries, we've cut the tree population nearly in half.

Today, annual tree harvest versus tree production on a global scale shows that humans cut down approximately 15 billion trees a year but only replant about 5 billion.

That's a net loss of 10 billion trees on average per year, decreasing natural weather systems, meaning less moisture transpired back into the air, meaning less rain, less growth, less food, less medicine, less shelter and way more desert.

We install vertical trellises for climbing ivy species over unused outdoor wall surfaces, where perennial vines could easily grow. Sure, rats like to use those as ladders sometimes, that's why the trellises will always stop at least a few feet before the top of a wall. Worried about structural damage to your wall from the climbing plants? Worry not: we can use textile netting made from recycled ocean plastics to keep the plants off the walls, minimising structural damage. We procure the materials for these nets to be made from Plastic Bank, a company who have turned plastic into literal money in impoverished countries.

Cool-looking funnel-mouthed tanks are installed on rooftop corners to catch rainwater, to be dispersed through the green walls via simple recycled plastic pipe irrigation systems.

We plan and dig small corridors out of the concrete and asphalt, so that they could be landscaped with fast-growing Miyawaki mini-forests, and maintained with little maintenance.

We create criss-crossing hedgerow corridors for animal life over long stretches through towns.

We mobilise groups of people who are wearied by climate anxiety, and who are into planting stuff, to re-plant and do some maintenance on a few weekends in the spring and autumn.

We create community projects around the new trees, shrubs and hedgerows. We reach out to educational bodies and get the students involved. Take them out on field trips to demonstrate the real joy of planting things in the ground and watching them grow, allowing them to make a genuine mark on their town's landscape.

We utilise commercial outlet rooftops as flower, bird and bee sanctuaries. God knows, these days there are plenty of gigantic commercial outlets in Portlaoise. The newer shopping areas are big, ugly, grey, American-style strip malls with vast amounts of parking. They are a real concrete experience, and yet, wherever I go in the world, Ireland's reputation for being a lush and green country is always the one that precedes it.

We encourage homeowners who are bored of their labour-intensive grass lawns to convert to clover or grass-and-clover lawns. Clover lawns are hugely good for biodiversity. Clover lives in poor soil and is resistant to drought, so stays way greener than grass all summer. It is delightfully soft and spongy underfoot. It adds nitrogen to the soil, improving its health, and attracts bees. Clover can also be crushed and drunk as tea. It has been used as medicine since forever, as menopausal relief, to improve hair and skin and as a remedy for asthma and arthritis. My mate Pablo has a clover lawn in front of his house. He only has to cut it twice a year, it stays looking great all year round, and when he walks out in the morning barefoot, butterflies spring up from the ground and flutter and swirl all around him.

If you are a farmer, landscaping strips of Miyawaki mini-forest along the edges and a few strips down the middle of the fields would not only help win your town a Green Town Award, but would also create lots of wild animal habitats and greatly improve the fertility of the soil.

Agroforestry is a fascinating new/old science. Agroforestry is the combination of agricultural, pastoral (grazing animals) and forestry elements together. Trees are planted amongst the crops either in rows, grids or random, and then goats/sheep/cows breeze through and eat and shit everywhere. This improves the soil's micro-climate, increases soil fertility and prevents water and wind erosion. It also provides better shelter for livestock and homes for many other species.

There is no objective reason why the provision of food has to equal the decimation of our sources of air, cooling, biodiversity and animal habitats. Why rip out our earth-to-air moisture cables (trees) instead of coming up with a way of having our cake (trees) and eating well too? There are many mouths to feed and currently we are not feeding enough of them, but it seems absurd to accept that the way we feed ourselves en masse must contribute to the accelerating destruction of the planet.

In the documentary *Kiss the Ground*, Woody Harrelson ominously presents us with this: based on the annihilated bacteria population in farmed soil due to the constant use of poisonous chemicals, America now has only about sixty harvests left. After that, desertification. The soil turns to dirt which turns to dust, and then it's millions more of us living on land where you can grow fuck-all.

Desertification leads to intensified food insecurity, which leads to more extreme decisions being made, which leads to the rolling back of human rights, which leads to conflict. We've seen this play out before.

The farmers are the ones who produce the food, so they get to choose. The decision to change the way we grow is ultimately up to them, and it won't be easy. Small ideas written down become a very large-scale thing to fully realise. To run the risk by changing up how he and his forebears have always done things? And it's hard, because if a farmer is not a corporation but produces for a corporation, he may live season to season. And the pesticides and fertilisers he uses to run the farm, so far, have worked every time.

Maybe the stagnated changeover of food production is not because farmers refuse to read the writing on the wall, but because they're not in a position to take the financial risk. They don't have much room to experiment with new growing techniques that, sure, address climate damage, but may make their farm go tits-up in the short term.

This is why at governmental level, we must seriously get on with the provision of subsidy/encouragement to catalyse the changeover to more sustainable food production practices. Practices which already exist. It's not like humanity is toiling desperately waiting for them to be invented. Granted, the agroforestry concept needs more research to be taken seriously in the modern world, but it is the future of food production, where the land becomes a credit to the climate again, not just another burden.

The European Green Deal is an allegedly €7 trillion-backed new agency tasked with making Europe the first carbon-neutral continent and the leader in the great climate transition to fully sustainable food production. In its mission, it doesn't mention anything about agroforestry specifically, but it does say:

> Organic farming is an environmentally friendly practice that needs to be further developed. The Commission will boost the development of EU organic farming area with the aim to achieve 25 per cent of total farmland under organic farming by 2030.

This is the open door, needed in America and Asia too, so that our friends who we rely on in food production can walk through it if they so choose.

But before we lose the run of ourselves altogether, for this Green Town Awards to work we'd need to start small, by picking a few trial spots around town.

We begin with trialling the increase of Miyawaki mini-forests around healthcare nucleuses like hospitals, hospices and palliative-care facilities, since it has been proven by Roger Ulrich, a professor of healthcare design, that 'patients with a green view [out their hospital room window] need less medication and are discharged sooner after surgery than those who don't have a window or whose room looks out on a wall'.

Next, we spiral the small corridors around educational facilities. Creches, play schools, schools, universities. And then, eventually, to places where large amounts of us work and recreate.

Perhaps, then, the Midlands Regional Hospital in Portlaoise is the ideal place to start with this carbon capture template. It was, after all, where I was born. And there is plenty of exterior wall space and surrounding land to play with.

Or perhaps Portlaoise Town Hall, right in the centre, would be a great place to start. Those big bare walls and surrounding shaved lawnlettes are oozing with potential. The one and only time I've ever entered that building was when I was eleven-ish years old, as the Irish trad music accompaniment to some function that was taking place on the top floor. My most vivid memory about that night was this other wily, long-haired musician fellow who I didn't recognise. He played the bouzouki, a long-necked Greek lute-style instrument, but most importantly he was wearing bright yellow jeans. I couldn't believe my eyes.

Or, how about the Garda (police) station property across the road from there? My dad's former office, with its great big bare boundary walls and oodles of potential space? Where we used to waste whole afternoons as kids playing snooker in the games room and eating chocolate bars and crisps out of the vending machine.

Or the GAA clubhouse and pitches further out the Abbeyleix Road. Where Portlaoise FC once reigned victorious over Mountmellick as Laois County Champions Under-14s with a certain young Sheehan wreaking havoc up in the corner forward position.

Or Portlaoise Prison, the largest prison in Ireland. I grew up right next to it but have never set foot inside. Never say never. Famously, prison food is not the most nutritious or tasty in the world, so why not give inmates the opportunity to grow and maintain some of their own?

Or the old courthouse on the cobbled Main Street. Lots of surface area to play with there.

Or the Dunamaise Arts Centre right next door, whose boards I first trod playing a forest pixie in a pantomime version of *Red Riding Hood*. I remember the smell of Red Riding Hood's perfume. Banana-y. And the biggest laugh we got the whole run was when JP misspoke his line 'There are pixies in the woods' by saying 'There are pixies in the wolf,' and then couldn't pull himself together and stop laughing. The audience roared. The thrill of watching something going wrong onstage.

Or perhaps for our Green Town Awards trial it will end up being a business owner who believes in the idea and can see its simplicity, so they donate some outdoor wall or roof space to the environment. Maybe we have a big flashy Grand Opening on their premises.

Lastly, not only do I publicly propose to co-create the Green Town Awards, but also to pay for it. On the condition that Portlaoise County Council match the funds. Hmmm . . .

RESULT! Within ten years, Portlaoise boasts a significant and measurable increase in its native biodiversity. Everybody's mood improves, everybody breathes cleaner air, and our lungs are stronger which means our chests all hang a little looser.

In County Laois, too many of us are dying by suicide every year, particularly men. Because of this, many are justifiably calling for an increase in mental health resources to help reverse the tide. But isn't it interesting how now, with the verified scientific proof that increasing the concentration of biodiverse plantlife around us increases our physical and mental health, we have the opportunity to make a lateral impact on the lives of so many? It will happen in incremental parts, the sum of which will amount to a far greater whole.

This idea is too simple, possible and cost-effective not to at least trial. Come on, Portlaoise, let's be the first.

I often thought that if Ireland were to reunify in my lifetime, the relief would be like my sound healing class in Bali; the release of trapped energy from a chakra the size of the whole country.

Letting go of pain we'd forgotten was there because we'd gotten so used to it. The Green Town Awards would recognise Ireland as one country. And extend the invitation north of the border so that together, we all re-tree our one country as one community.

I can see it now. The smiling Green Town Courier in a floppy cap and brightly coloured trainers sticks the invitation in the elasticated waistband of his joggers and makes a beeline as the crow flies across Cavan to the border of Fermanagh. The first man he encounters on the other side is driving a tractor. So he hops the gate and sprints across the field waving the waxen-sealed letter in the air. The Fermanagh farmer cuts his engine and sits wide-eyed looking out the windscreen at the Courier, waving an envelope wildly with his outstretched arm as he reaches the tractor door. He doubles over, catches his breath and, grinning from ear to ear, hands it over. The farmer reads it and looks up:

'I'll give you thirty seconds to get off my lond.'

Ah Ireland, God Bless her, in time may she return to being one country again after over a hundred years of being split in two.

By the time I got home from my *ohm*-walk, it had become spring. The ground was thawing and life was waking up in my little patch of garden. Not since I'd lived back in the homeplace in Portlaoise had I had a bit of land to play with, but when I lived there I was a child and didn't give a bollocks about gardening.

Did you know that the human voice boosts plant growth? Optimally around the 70-decibel mark, which is the average human conversational volume.

The Royal Horticultural Society did a month-long study involving ten gardeners. Each participant read a book to a tomato plant daily. All of them grew larger than the control plants. But the ones that experienced female voices were an inch taller than those with male talkers. Plants after my own heart.

It may be the sonic vibration of the voice, or the carbon-dioxide emitted in a human's breath required by the tomato plant for photosynthesis, or maybe a combination of the two.

Sometimes, I spread rumours around my garden, muttering to some rocket leaves, 'Here, see that tomato plant over there? I heard him calling ye cuntsss . . .'

For me, growing food is comparable to seeing the night sky out in the countryside. In that it feels like something essential to me that was previously removed from view my whole life.

Putting a seed of something in a pot, and then a little sapling appearing as if by magic, smiling up at you like a delicate green satellite of hope. 'Doo-do-doo, *bon soir*, Planty.'

And then, the satisfaction earned from harvesting the food, and the fact that it is ten times tastier and more nutritious than any of the mass-produced stuff in the shop. Here's a little nutrition test at the grocery store: hold fresh produce three inches from your nose and see if you can smell it.

I sent my friend Jy home with some sweet basil, and he said the whole train carriage could smell it in his backpack on the way home.

And I give no credence to this notion of a 'green thumb'. It doesn't reflect the true nature of it. It's more of an 'If at first you don't succeed, try and try again' situation: practice makes progress, like everything else in this world. The thumb turns green after a little trial and murder.

I can see myself now as an old man, with the whole beige gardening kit and caboodle on. Sun-hat, kerchief and khaki shorts, barefoot and crouched, trowelling away in some patch of dirt listening to the Vengaboys' greatest hits. Green edible life exploding everywhere, and birdsong, and the lovely voiced hum of insectoids.

If I make it that far.

Here is another interesting technique for you to play with, one that I have found very effective.

Like all my other favourite things, candles poison you just a little. I've always loved the crackle of a dying candle. If you're also a fan of burning candles at home, you'll enjoy this one. This technique is called *tratak*, which is a Sanskrit word roughly meaning 'to gaze'. It's a yogic technique to unify the body and mind, and is practised with eyes open.

I have been watching other people's eyes in public, which, if you're not careful, can land you in hot water. How their eyes sit still. How quickly they move about. If they dart around and stray from place to place, barely taking a moment to register what they're seeing before leaping to the next place, they are windows that suggest inside them a restless soul. And it's like the person is somehow less there, lost behind a fog of fast-moving impulses. The darting eyes suggest a soul who is less aware, because their awareness is stretched so thin.

But when the eyes are at rest and sit more still, it's like the whole world feels superfluous around them. And that the world is being created for them, by them.

They are expanded awareness, devoting its focus to whatever thing the eyes are pointing at. The true paydirt is seeing eyes that are looking out, but behind them you can tell the mind is really looking in. Aware of some awareness of some activity of itself.

The technique of *tratak* is to bring the eyes gently to rest on a fixed point. It can be a dot on the wall, but I've always found a flickering, flirtatious candle flame infinitely more interesting.

Tratak makes use of the strong connection between the eye and the mind.

Learning to rest the eyes there, fixed on one point, without strain, rests and clarifies the mind. It has also been shown to be very effective at improving focus and concentration, and as a result of this, improving the memory over time. Some advocates even report improvements in their eyesight as a result of the muscles around their eyes getting stronger.

I went with my love on our first silent meditation retreat.

There was a thirst in us both for pilgrimage. We were inescapably drawn, as flowers are drawn to light, to a place that could provide respite from all the usual running and racing, so that we could have a good long contemplation undisturbed.

The retreat was a five-days-and-nights affair. It was designed to be a gentler Vipassana-style retreat, which typically goes on for ten. And to be a first step for beginners who have never observed prolonged silence before.

Before taking the train out of Valencia, we rushed around the city, excitedly gathering supplies of loose-fitting pants, foam muscle rollers, notepads and pens, torches for seeing at night, and earplugs for all the snoring bastards we'd be sleeping beside. And, concerned about all the sitting on the ground we'd be required to do, I used the hour's train journey to stretch on the floor and lambast myself with a spiky foam roller, which, it transpired, was tantamount to 'sharpening the sword after the battle had begun', to quote Mr DeVaney, my English teacher from school.

We were picked up from the station in an old Spanish monastery town, bundled into a couple of vans, and driven way out the country.

The other silence-seekers came in from all over Europe, and as we zoomed past fields and fields of orange groves, we chit-chatted in the van.

There was the lawyer whose marriage had hit the skids, the son who still lived at home in the oppressive air of an anxious father, the young lady leather tramp (someone who travels around in a van) who'd been exploring different ways of coping with depression, the scientist who'd become deeply bored and disillusioned with her job in the laboratory, and the tall young rake who, as soon as we arrived on site, was already talking about getting back to the city and going on the beer. And there was us, the couple who were head over heels, but struggling.

Our destination lay tucked away on a narrow tract of land, which snaked along the foot of some rocky mountains to the south-east. All around us were the groves. Fiercely symmetrical rows and rows of plump little orange trees. And, once the silence got going, those of us observing it would wander reclusively in those groves, like patients let out of the psychiatric ward for their daily walk.

When you go on a silent meditation retreat, the service they are really providing you with is creating a space and a routine so that you have to think as little as possible. We were awoken at quarter past six by the gentle tinging of a Tibetan singing bowl, we were fed vegetarian breakfast, lunch and dinner, and were herded into a circular Mongolian-style yurt to practise silent stillness every other hour or so by a little ringing brass bell.

I decided to approach the whole thing as a kind of vacation – why not? 'This is going to be nice and relaxing!' I thought to myself. 'I don't have to talk to anyone, I just have to be there and take part in lots of long, luxurious-with-a-slice-of-lemon medita tions, which I love doing anyway.' What could possibly go wrong?

What I failed to anticipate was that the joy of not talking to anyone for days on end also meant the hell of talking incessantly to myself. I came up with a unique retreat mantra. A short and snappy *ohm*, to be rolling away in my chest as soon as I awoke, to get the jump on my frantic morning mind, and to replace the newsreel of thinking, so that I could try to remain present with (the rest of) myself throughout the day.

If practising inward contemplation was a search engine, like Ecosia or Google, instead of typing something into the searchbar, my aim was to leave it blank and click 'search' anyway.

Those of not us sleeping in their own vans were housed in another circular Mongolian-style yurt adjacent, containing bunk-beds enough for us two loves and eight others. The yurt also had a wood-burning stove and chimney column in its centre, which was never lit.

The only correspondence the two of us shared was via little folded pieces of paper left under each other's pillows, which contained doodles, poems and declarations of love. We'd sneak them into their hiding places to await discovery, like political prisoners in a minimum-security canvas-walled prison. She was always first up and out, and by the time the rest of us rose, her bed was already made. And my heart would go frantic wondering where she'd gone and what she was up to.

Our days consisted of light morning yoga, four or five good group meditations, discourses on the teachings of Buddha, and long walks in single file through the magnificent beautiful hills that the sun would peak out from behind at exactly eleven fifteen in the morning. There were no clocks, but there was a schedule, and it was interesting how quickly I learned to tell the time by where the sun was in the sky. On that tract of land, by the end of day two I could guess it right down to the accuracy of about ten minutes either side.

There was the odd evening sound-healing class too, but I fell asleep in all of them, and snored like the shutters being slammed closed on a shopfront (apparently).

And there were volunteers helping to facilitate our silence while living on the land and working for their keep. The WWOOFer types, who drift from place to place earning bed and board. I could definitely see myself as one of those people had I not found an alternative means of paid travel.

Days one and two were just fine. The vacation was going well. It felt easy. I prematurely thought, 'I'm in good shape here! My personal purposelessness practice has indeed given me power enough over my mind to where even a vow of silence can't knock me off my stride.' And I was sleeping like a log. My circadian rhythm quickly fell in step with the cosmos. By the time the sun was falling, I could barely keep my eyes open.

Then, on day three, the vacation ended and things got challenging. Despite my *ohm* rolling, the noise inside my head steadily increased, until on that third day it reached fever pitch and I was consumed. Deprived of the usual soothers of everyday life, denied the usual familiar pattern, my mental static got so loud that I lost all ability to be present with myself.

There was an interesting neurological study done out of the Centre for Neuroscience Studies in Queen's University, Canada on mental cognition, which was published in the scientific journal *Nature Communications*. Using a brain scan machine called an fMRI, Dr Jordan Poppenk and Julie Tseng wanted to answer the question of, 'How does consciousness flow from one spontaneous thought to the next?'

Instead of trying to study the thoughts themselves or their contents, they focussed on studying the transitional periods between thoughts. This turned out to be a useful measure in demarcating thoughts from one another, and they could estimate that an average mind has about 6,000 spontaneous thoughts per day. By day three of the retreat, I felt like that number had leapt to 50,000.

Buddha called our innate propensity to passively secrete thoughts our 'monkey mind'. Because its behavioural pattern, straying from tree to tree, leaping erratically from one thought to the next, reflects the behaviour of a monkey, obviously. Mind's activity is animal in nature, a nature that is being watched by Us, the Overseers.

My monkey mind was chattering and hopping louder than he ever had, and I fell blindly out of awareness and into the torrent stream of thoughts. As a response to this, when we weren't in the yurt practising quiet stillfulness, I unconsciously reverted to my old tactics of trying to *suppress* the noise, to *switch it off*, by trying to replace the noise with shallow feelings of completionism. Completionism meaning a temporary, shallow state of happiness gained from completing some task. For me that meant writing some pages in my journal, clocking more hours practising meditation on my own, or stretching.

I have a tendency to feel useless if I am not achieving stuff. My sense of self-esteem is interwoven with the notion of productivity. But this compulsion to always be productive pervades my leisure time, and in this case contemplation time. Left unchecked, it gets to the point where it becomes impossible to attain to a real, satisfactory state of contentment, because my mindset is propelled forward by the cattleprod of completionism, which denies me happiness in the moment in exchange for the delayed pleasure of ticking a box to say that I have completed a task. It is only a temporary, unsustainable form of happiness, the happiness of 'getting things done'.

By day three among us souls observing the silence together, wandering around in our own reclusive consciousnesses, there was a ripe old rate of resting bitch face, me included, not that there were any mirrors. But I didn't need one to know because the volume inside my head had become unreasonable. And somewhere forgotten under the rubble of all that mental static was that most important aspect of contemplation/self-enquiry: *Ahimsa*. In other words, I'd fallen down a deep well of self-criticism, where I could neither move nor sit still. I felt trapped, under an increasing weight of despair. And looking back now, I am grateful to my monkey. Because by rattling the branches and screeching and throwing bananas, he left my present heart (me) no choice. And this is how prolonged silence taught me that my heart can speak. Just like how my monkey mind 'speaks' of past and future – got to do this, got to do that, should have done this, should be doing that – my heart speaks only from the present. And not only does my heart speak, it is in fact the one who is in charge of all the others: the monkey mind, the hunger pig, the craving tiger, the libido dormouse. My head had been acting up wildly to get the heart's (my) attention, like I did with my mother when I was a child, or my dog, Rory, does when he's bored. And the truth behind all its noise, what my monkey was really screaming for, was help. He was frantically begging me, the present heart, for a little loving instruction, for some establishment of a new order in this unfamiliar retreat regime.

And when I wasn't actively responding with authority, when his cries were repeatedly falling on deaf ears, his only recourse was to get louder and louder until he was heard. In that noisy silence, I learned something fundamental about the nature of my mind. How it speaks not just to be heard, but also to be told. It is the monkey, and the present heart (me) is the organ grinder. I'd always wondered what an organ grinder was: organ grinders, in ye olde times, were street entertainers who played barrel organs, and sometimes had a monkey trained to dance along to the music.

So, during a long, creamy indoor contemplation in the sun-blessed grass under an orange tree, I lovingly spoke to my dancing monkey. Firstly, I acknowledged his presence: 'I see you, and I hear you. Thank you.' And then, just like that time spent shuffling around alone on the *Endgame* stage, by embracing my present heart's voice, that one we employ to inwardly say the mantra, I gave my mind some new, direct instruction.

And when this worked, when on day four my internal storm responded by relaxing right down to a calm, still sea, I realised how I had lived so much of life back-to-front! How I'd laboured unnecessarily under the illusion that the human condition is such that when thoughts occur they occur, and there is nothing much anyone can do about that. But in fact, the opposite is true. The monkey mind's incoherence is subject to the instruction of a *realistic* present heart's voice. I say 'realistic' because, of course, I don't claim that one can will the mind never to think. This would be equally as pointless as asking your toenails not to grow. For the mind 'secretes thoughts the way the salivary gland secretes saliva', according to Jack Kornfield, Buddhist teacher.

But it is possible to enter into a meaningful, respectful dialogue with the mind, one where you hold most of the cards at the table.

This was not the first time in life that I was backed into a corner by the chattering monkey and forced to resort to the power of positive affirmation.

I was sixteen years old, making television in Vancouver. A daytime action-adventure effort about a new generation of the three musketeers called *Young Blades*. I played Louis the Dauphin, the king of France, in a big powdered wig and pantaloons.

And because I was still only the tender age of sixteen, I was placed under the tutelage of one of the production managers who worked in the office, Denise. For six months I lived with her, her partner Sam, her son (can't remember) and her cat, also named Sam. Sam the human was charming, but Sam the cat bit and scratched me so many times I became allergically averse to cats for life (thus far). Outside of the filming and daily on-set school tutoring, I was *profoundly* lonely. I would despondently wander the vacant suburban neighbourhood streets at night, listening to the same four gloomy albums over and over on a broken MP3 player (broken in that I'd managed to get those four albums onto it, but after that it refused to take on any other music).

On set, I'd be trying to act cooler than I was, with actors who were all at least ten years older than me. And that's when the monkey-mind impostor would go the hardest: when I was around the ones I most wanted to like me.

'OK, Karen's just mentioned skiing. Now, we went on a skiing trip with school last year. Good! Good, let's talk about that the next time there's an opening to talk. Hang on, wait for it . . . Wait . . . Hang on, wait . . . Wait . . . OK, now!'

But of course, by the time Karen had finished what she was saying, and it was my opportunity to contribute my little pearl which I'd been fiercely holding on to instead of listening, not only had the conversation moved on but the whole world had moved on with it. It was was so alarming and distracting, noticing the impostor emerging so forcefully to the point of planning out whatever I was going to say in advance.

And I mourned terribly for the times before, when I'd had the ability to just say things without having to plan them out internally.

At first, I just surrendered to the impostor. This stowaway in my brain trying to convince me that he was me. I keeled over and felt sad for the future.

There were days when I'd come loafing through Denise's front door with the inner dialogue racing: 'You're fucked. You've had sixteen years of childish fun but now, say goodbye to all that. That ship has sailed *for life*. You've gone quietly insane and you don't know how to talk about it with anyone else.'

Nobody had told me being an adult meant feeling like this. Many gloomy journal entries and angsty poems were written in that time in attempts to assuage the impostor's effects. Poor teen-age me, if only I'd read a book which explained that the express route back to my whole, uninterrupted self lay in simply listening to the other person. Or, if I was alone, simply listening to myself.

But then one day several months in, after one too many stilted and awkward conversations, I decided I'd had enough and stood up to myself. My stubborn little head declared: 'No, fuck this. I will not go gently into this good night. I refuse to take all this interference lying down! This impostor voice has not always been here so it has no right to stay. Nor does it have the right to barge in here unannounced and start calling the shots and ruining my life. You will not seize creative control that easy, my impostor friend. You might want to rabbit on, but I will fight the good fight for my younger self, because he was way more fun to exist inside of.'

I wanted to launch a counter-attack, but I didn't know how. So, in lieu of knowing, every time I had the presence of mind to notice the impostor palpitating away, I began silently ordering it to stop: 'Quiet, you! I've got this, thank you.'

Then, when this miniature rebellion began to show minor results, and my mind palpitations gradually began to at least temporarily obey and recede from view, it restored all sorts of confidence. I thought, 'Wow, if I have the power to positively affect this bullshit going on inside, then I can deal with anything going on on the outside.'

When this realisation dawned, I leapt up onto the roof of my trailer right in the middle of school tutoring, like Emilio Estevez after smoking all that weed in the foreign language room of *The Breakfast Club*. And I roared across the production unit base: 'I am an agent of the universe. I am the hand of god!' Or did I add that detail later for messianic effect?

Nowadays, it is easy to see the real reason for the impostor's appearance. I was only sixteen years of age, thousands of miles from home, and knew no one. I did not feel secure. I'd only ever known myself inside of a certain context.

I really do owe a huge debt of gratitude to the impostor, though. To the palpitating monkey mind, for the fact that it was the first positive affirmation I ever made – without possessing the frilly language 'positive affirmation' to describe it – and it was one that was forged out of pure, molten jeopardy. I'd been backed into a corner and left with no choice.

After that experience in Vancouver, I occasionally did a little *lokah samastah* – again without the Buddhist language *lokah samastah* to name it – to reaffirm to myself: 'I am fit and healthy. I am strong. I have no reason to fear anything.'

Variations to that effect. And in time, backed by the aggregate of experience, this became easier to believe. And through that belief, instead of looking to other things to give me strength, I became more the source of my own.

I must confess, though, Father . . . Since we are on the subject, sometimes the impostor still shows up unannounced. But now, it's easier to see it for what it is: a predictable reaction to an unfamiliar environment.

Back inside the Mongolian-style meditation yurt, we the group of silent ten, led by our teacher, Ellen, practised many, many hours of expansive quietness together. The cross-legged sitting was a hoor for me. I was forever fidgeting and readjusting my ass and back cushions, so that I could just let go and rest fully into the floor like a sack of rice. But frustratingly, I could never quite get fully comfortable. My misshapen hips, misshapen from a life spent sitting on chairs in schools and couches at home instead of on the ground, would not allow it. Thus, I was always subject to this needly pain up my back left side. So the meditations themselves were not as good as usual. I much preferred practising meditation by myself in the Spanish wintry sunny afternoon.

I have never been wild about wallowing in the watering hole of wonderfulness in a group scenario; I have always preferred to practise on my own. That way I can snuffle and grunt and fart and express myself in whatever fashion the watering hole requests. Whereas I've always found myself a bit inhibited by the presence of other people, and a bit less inclined to dive as deeply into myself as I usually would. That said, there were times in that yurt when I could palpably feel all of us beginning to resonate together at the same low vibration. That, in a fundamental sense, we became one. We became entrained onto the same bodily rhythm, and feelings were broadcast between one another without even trying. Like if you were to put ten grandfather clocks side by side and get all their pendulums swinging, their rhythms would naturally fall in step together. And even if you knocked one of the pendulums out of whack, so that it was swinging at a different frequency (meaning swings per second), its rhythm will naturally become entrained and fall back in step with the others all by itself. This is a natural law of the universe called rhythmic entrainment.

Together, we ten silent swingers (not in that way) shared awareness to expand into the territory that language cannot be put to. If I was to envision the sum of all human information exchange as an ocean, then verbal communication would be just on its surface, floating around like alphabetti spaghetti.

This experience of rhythmic entrainment reminded me of another natural law I learned about. A phenomenon that occurs when groups of people practise meditation together at a critical number, called the Maharishi effect.

But before we get into the the Maharishi effect, I must first briefly explain another natural law of the universe called the Meissner effect. The Meissner effect was a phenomenon discovered in 1933 by German physicists Walther Meissner and Robert Ochsenfeld.

The Meissner Effect is where all of the particles of an object, such as a piece of tin, lead, lithium or chrome, line themselves up in such a neat way that electrical energy can pass freely through the object with zero resistance or energy loss. When an object is employed in such a way, it is referred to as a conductor.

When a conductor is sufficiently cooled below its critical temperature, it becomes a superconductor, and only then does the Meissner effect occur: where the substance relaxes all of its electrical sensitivity down, and brings its subatomic particles to rest. Which creates a powerfully coherent magnetic current along the surface of the object, which in turn creates a kind of shield around the object. A shield which can block all other magnetic interference patterns, which might have been pinging around in the universe, from passing through it.

Superconducting magnets make the most powerful magnets in the world. They are ushering in a new era of land travel in the form of Maglev trains. Magnetic levitation trains can (currently) travel up to 500km per hour. They are quiet because there are no parts grinding together, which also makes derailment highly unlikely, and they produce little to no air pollution since no fuel is being burned. They run solely on magnetic power.

The discovery of the Meissner effect also made it possible to closely study the behaviour of the tiniest particles in our universe through something called nuclear magnetic resonance, or NMR. NMR is basically where an electrical turkey baster is shoved up into the centre of a superconductor magnet and squirts out sample molecules. It then zaps said molecules with little electric impulses. Very kinky stuff. The electrons of these molecules are the ones that, to quote Max Planck, '. . . [bring] the particles of an atom to vibration and [hold] this most minute solar system of the atom together'.

Electrons are the ones that orbit the nucleus of the atom. And they behave like magnets in a magnetic field. But, once they are steadied, once they are 'shielded' inside of the superconductor, their electrical signals become recordable and manipulatable.

Maharishi Mahesh Yogi, the man whose name was used to name the Maharishi effect, said this (in a funny high-pitched voice): 'The surface activity of the conscious mind deepens and incorporates within its fold the depth of the subconscious. And, with practice, nothing remains subconscious.'

Maharishi was a physicist and a spiritual teacher who became famous in America and Europe in the 1960s. He appeared on such magazine covers as *Time, Rolling Stone* and *Newsweek*. According to legend, Frank Oz based his iconic Yoda voice from *Star Wars* on Maharishi. In 1968, after the death of Brian Epstein, the Beatles visited Maharishi's ashram in Rishikesh, India. It proved to be a fruitful trip. They reportedly wrote (to some degree or other) forty-eight songs, and released *The White Album* later that year (an album which is really entitled *The Beatles*). But they left India on a sour note, and John later described Maharishi to his wife, Cynthia, as too preoccupied by 'public recognition, celebrities and money.'

Maharishi popularised on a Western scale the Transcendental Meditation or TM technique. There are many videos on YouTube of him describing in depth his TM technique: search 'How to Meditate – Maharishi Mahesh Yogi'.

He studied physics at the University of Allahabad, and theorised that human doings can create something comparable to the Meissner 'shielding' effect by practising meditation in groups. Instead of a very, very cold piece of tin, you have a room-temperature group of people all settling their atomic particles together, over a stretch of time.

He applied his theory through social science experiments, and his effect was proven to exist many times over in many different studies, and across over *fifty different cities* throughout the 1960s, 1970s and 1980s.

Every time they conducted this experiment over roughly a three-year period, and cross-referenced it against an equal number of control cities that were not carrying out the experiment, it yielded similar results.

In Merseyside, England, they conducted a Maharishi effect experiment from 1988 to 1992. The correlation between the city's behaviour rates and Maharishi group transcendental meditation sessions was carefully tracked and measured using a complex version of a simple statistical model known as a time series analysis. Complex time series analyses are what financial markets use to predict future economic growth and loss. A time series is an observation of values taken at regular intervals of time, say daily or weekly. In this case, the observations being recorded were the rates of group transcendental meditation sessions versus the city's rate of violent crime.

On the UK government's own website, in the Recorded Crime Statistics for England and Wales section, the total violence against the person rate goes from 158,248 incidents in 1988, to 201,777 in 1992. Which is a reported increase of over 27 per cent. And yet –

'The crime rate fell by 16 per cent in Merseyside, whereas during the same period it increased by 20 per cent in the rest of England and Wales. Merseyside moved from the third highest crime rate of all metropolitan areas in the UK to the second lowest. There were 170,000 fewer crimes in Merseyside than expected over the 3.5 year experimental period, and the projected savings to the government was 850 million British pounds.'

G.D. Hatchard, A.J. Deans, K. Cavanaugh, and D.W. Orme-Johnson,
Maharishi International University

Not only that, but the effect turned out to be a hole that was exponentially larger than the sum of its parts. During March of 1988, there occurred a whopping 13.4 per cent increase in orderliness and harmony and a drop in crime, which corresponded exactly to the time when the Merseyside Maharishi effect test group finally got to a size where it was equal in number to the square root of 1 per cent of the population of Merseyside. Just as Maharishi had theorised that it would. I wonder if the experiment taking place in Merseyside in Liverpool had anything to do with his previous arguments with the Beatles . . .

By practising 'yogic flying', a technique devised by Maharishi called TM-Sidhi, where everyone hops along the cushioned floor cross-legged looking a bit silly, a group the size of the square root of 1 per cent of the whole Merseyside population made that level of positive impact on violent crime. In 1988, Merseyside's population was just under 1 million and falling slowly. So, in those three and a half years, as the UK's overall violent crime rate rocketed by a whopping 20–25 per cent according to the sources above, the group number who made a 13–16 per cent *improvement* on the rate of Merseyside's violent crime rate was 122.47 people. That is a spectacularly achievable number.

Off the back of these amazing results, in March 1992 Maharishi went into politics, forming the Natural Law Party in the UK. His mission was not only to align his body more deeply with the universe's optimum tempo, but also to align the body of society.

'As individual consciousness grows, collective consciousness rises; and as collective consciousness rises, individual consciousness grows. Individual

consciousness is the basic unit of all levels of
collective consciousness – family
consciousness, community consciousness,
national consciousness and world
consciousness – influencing them all and
being in turn influenced by them.'

Maharishi Mahesh Yogi

This was an incredibly interesting move. He was the first individual that I'm aware of to attempt to take the benefits of practising meditation personally and apply them, in the UK or elsewhere, politically.

The Natural Law Party's policies were based on Transcendental Meditation and the laws of quantum physics, and its mission was, according to its leader, Geoffrey Clements, 'to bring the intelligence of nature into the field of government'.

Their stated aims were to create fully clean energy, remove air pollution, reintroduce fully sustainable farming practices and pull the UK out of the foreign arms trade. They were quite well funded and contested 310 seats in the 1992 UK general election, but won exactly zilch.

How about Ireland though, for the craic? According to Worldometer, as of 2024, Ireland's population is just over 5 million people.

One per cent of 5 million is 50,000, and the square root of 50,000 is 223.6 people.

Let's round that figure up to 250.

So if you had a group of, say, 500 to 1,000 rotating people, taking days on and days off, to make sure that there definitely were

250 people communing in meditation together every day, that would be more than enough to cover it. And what would happen if we doubled that figure? So that it was a group of 250 people, say, in two different locations on the island?

Over the space of three years we would generate the Maharishi effect, and would experience a considerable increase in harmony and a measurable reduction in societal stress comparable to the Merseyside experiment.

Interesting, eh? Who's up for it?

When we put our heads together in peace, we have the power to amplify the power of nationwide consciousness. Promoting calm, love, integrity and safety for all. All we have to do is get together and return our minds to the natural process of things.

This is a new and unexplored frontier for humanity because it is an idea of unknown potential. One which to try will, at its very least, relax and improve people's overall health, and at its most has the potential to bring about a global renaissance.

To play around with meditation on a society-wide scale is an idea that chimes deeply in both my heart and my reason, despite my disdain for practising around other people.

The logistics of this plan are so simple. Sure, it seems a little bizarre at first, but who cares about that? Evidence shows that it works. It is an act of generosity and democracy, because it affects every soul within its shield equally. And generating an impenetrable shield of peacefulness sounds way less boring than having to go to Mass.

I bet if the Irish government put a tiny, microscopic fraction of their budget aside to enact a scheme, based on evidence-based scientific research, that actively encourages us to practise meditation together and take a meaningful role in our community's safety and prosperity, not just for ourselves but for each other, then large numbers of us would likely apply. Imagine how good we'd make them look.

Far be it from me to imagine sitting on a quiet contemplation carriage on the train. One carriage set aside specifically for travelers moving through the city in meditation together, spreading calmness while communing with their fellow commuters on a level that requires no words.

Or strolling through central London first thing on a Monday morning, as the sun beams golden across thousands of city dwellers all sitting and resonating together in Trafalgar Square. All in/ as spaciousness, letting their individual selves gently dissolve into the fold together. Not absorbing news media or spending money or trying to get somewhere.

Warmed, not just by the sun, but also by the knowing that they are not only improving their own health, but they are also measurably helping to make their city a safer place to live. And warmed by the tingly satisfaction that they have started their week by positively contributing to the mood, friendliness and relaxation of millions of people they've never met, but with whom they share resources, towns, cities and a planet. And by the comfort, no doubt, in helping to keep their loved ones safe from afar.

Imagine the levels of social cohesion this simple reassignment of public space would inspire. And when everyone disperses after an hour and goes back to their lives, they naturally emanate this resonant calmness into their own individual worlds.

What if folks had a cornerstone in every big town and city? To press the flesh of their thumbs into. An open door where anyone can go, any day of the week, for the purposes of sheer purposelessness, and to return all the value of the world back to being.

A sermonless cornerstone of society, something completely unstuffy – in fact, let's just design it now.

Cornerstone Centre:

Rule 1: All rules can be broken.

Rule 2: Silence (we do our best).

Rule 3: Wear something baggy (if you show up stinking, you will be given some spare clothes and a bar of soap and you must have a quick shower or a sink wash).

Rule 4: Pay whatever you want.

Rule 5: Crying is an admirable way to break Rule 2 (crying, not wailing).

Rule 6: That's it.

It's a nice centre that's heated all year round. It holds three (up to) one-hour meditation sessions per day. Two just regular sitting still, and one of yogic flying.

It's got nice soft furnishings: pillows, cushions, mats, clean blankets and nice chairs. It caters to all levels, ages and flexibilities. In the evening sessions, it has warm twinkly lights and it's decorated with paintings and sculptures from local people who were inspired by the creative state they entered into by taking part. It's got a water cooler, lots of plants and natural light. Small trees grow in pots in the corners and plants dangle lazily from pots hanging from the ceiling. It smells of woody essential oils like pine, spruce, lavender and sandalwood. Up the front sits a friendly facilitator. And as you file in, you can see a selection of some encouraging sound-makers in front of them, like Tibetan singing bowls and tuning forks and gongs (I'm basically describing the sound-healing experience I had in Bali now).

It's welcome to one and all, and you can leave or come in (quietly) any time.

Each session begins with a nod, a smile or a hug with the person sitting next to you, a few deep breaths at the ring of a bell or a bowl, and off we go. And that's it.

We have evidence enough now to create a kind of NATO, but opposite. Peace NATO. Maharishi spent the latter part of his life trying to set this very thing up. He called it the Global Country of World Peace, where as well as nations having to come together to deliberate over the possibility of war, they also come together to actively consolidate peace. To go on the peace offensive.

There have been five known extinction events on this planet. But the next predicted extinction event is unique because it will be the first of its kind to be caused by the planet's dominant species. And yet, we are, as neurologist meditator Sam Harris put it, 'just climbing out of the darkness'.

If we stay on the track we're on, we accelerate blindly into our own annihilation. Which is terrifying, and sad, and for why? When we have such potential in our reserves to help restore this planet to its natural balance, and lose nothing. And to reclaim our species' disastrous self-image back from a juggernaut killer force to a nourishing steward. Imagine a bonkers world where we, the human doings, were actually proud of our contribution?

The show must go on. From the moment before death, to the moment of death, to the next moment after death, life barely notices your departure from the stage.

Our children we've never met are here in the blink of an eye, and they're wearing our old shoes ironically. And they are hot, very hot. Their feet are sweating, their skin is burning, their air is thinning and they're struggling to breathe.

They are feeling a legacy of neglect. They're fighting a losing battle against droughts and science-fiction-level hurricanes. They're warring with each other over previously fertile lands due to rapidly spreading deserts, exploding numbers of displaced people, human exploitation, political extremism and all the other fun stuff too.

Our species's recent history of material prosperity, brought about by advances in technology, has created an opposing starvation of spirit. And now, they are fighting not for an honourable cause or even a sense of peace and contentment, but for their family's next bite.

A natural law is defined by Merriam-Webster as, 'a body of law or a specific principle held to be derived from nature'.

All significant human progress has been achieved on the basis of scientific discovery: demonstrating the existence of a natural law of the universe, and then having your theory withstand the scrutiny of time.

Just like the law of gravity, the Maharishi effect is a demonstrable law. So why not see how much advantage we can take of it? If we are to have a real chance at multiplanetary prosperity, let's amplify the forces of love and cooperation. As the mystic Terence McKenna asked: 'Are we an episode in the biology of this planet, or will we build an Eden strung along the Milky Way?'

An important key to the power of our collective consciousness has been discovered. Let's see what doors it opens.

Back on the silent retreat, it was day four of five and I was sat on my Toblerone under an olive tree. The lovely bright Spanish sun had gone westward beyond the mountains as far as about three o'clock in the afternoon, and I was sitting in deep godfulness facing directly into it. There are few greater pleasures in life than sitting in a deep meditation while facing directly into the sun. By this point I was fully settled, and quite content in complete silence.

Bathed in the waning afternoon light, I filled up my body with plenty of oxygen and closed my eyes to see if I could let fully go of the sensation of my form.

It is an interesting experiment, to try to fully let go of form in meditation.

Surveying the sum of the energy field of my body, through the exhale I let it billow away like a mist. Replacing it with space, or you could say, embodying the space in its absence.

It was interesting because this revealed more specifically which parts of my form I find it hardest to physically let go of. For me, it's my face. My brow hangs on as steadfastly as it can. Exhaling lets the sensation of my face fall away, but it returns stubbornly like the tide a few seconds later.

I have always received compliments about my eyes, that I have nice eyes, and so they cling on pretty strongly to my sense of self. I find them difficult to let go of. Clingingess is a sensation that is instantly knowable. While you've been reading, in your own self-reflection sessions have you noticed which parts of your form are most clingy?

So there I was, basking in the sunset, letting it all go, when I was hit with an extraordinary revelation. It became clear as day that the way I had been perceiving reality was wrong, and that there is no such thing as time.

I'd always believed that I existed on a linear timeline. But really, there is only space, motion and memory.

Space is the amber that encases the infinite now in which we all reside.

Motion gives us the sense that time is 'passing', but actually none is. Things are just moving. Causing light to become dark, dark to become light, and causing the trees to lose their leaves or the trees to regrow their leaves. Causing that feeling when you look out your window and your whole street is covered in snow. Or you wake up and the sun is bursting through the bedroom window.

And the memory part is what presents us with a collection of snapshots of the various configurations of the moving objects around us, through a combination of sensorial, conceptual and emotional sensations, which flicker in and out of the now of moving space.

Lying there in the paradise sun, cradled in the symphony of the birds, whenever I felt mental time 'pop in', my heart spoke gently: 'No, thank you. For now, I'll just stick with space and motion, please.' And the linear time branch of my being dissolved.

Now, before I had flopped down on the grass under the olive tree, we had been exercising. We'd done a good solid session of lively yoga, and it felt so good I'd carried on my own little workout outside. As a result, my body was now coarsing with thrilling levels of dopamine, which I believe is key to what happened next. High levels of the hormone dopamine in our system is linked with feeling great.

At this point, for some unknown reason, a talk I'd once heard by the teacher Mooji floated into my mind. In his delicious, velvety voice, he spoke about that which perceives all. In other words, the seeingness, the third eye, this mysterious window of awareness that we all walk around being into. And how that which perceives all cannot itself be perceived. The all-seeing eye cannot itself be perceived because it is the one doing the perceiving, not the other way around. So, being a contrarian to the bitter end, and always up for a challenge, I began gently guiding my inner effort towards attempting to perceive that which was perceiving.

In the sunny darkness, I very softly zoomed out the lens of my perception, the I (eye), as far as I could make it go. Employing inner influence to broaden the perimeter of my spatial darkness. Determined to lovingly expend an extra *micro* effort to try to sense even more of the space around myself from further back.

Little did I know, but this was creating the perfect conditions for an out-of-body experience.

While this was going on, a light breeze rustled through the leaves above me and, in memory, what happened next has been saved conceptually as detaching and falling backwards 'out of' my body. In this moment, all physical and mental perceptions of form ceased, and I, that which was perceiving, very much remained. It felt like an unbodying experience. I once heard death described as 'taking off an overly tight shoe', and that is the most accurate description of this experience in words.

And it wasn't that I was now 'nothing'; it was that it had become abundantly clear that I am fundamentally everything, while temporarily experiencing a version of myself through this human manhole.

I couldn't tell you for how long my little death elapsed. How long in Earth spacetime I remained suspended, swaddled there, blissfully suckling from the teat of universal love. But when I re-emerged back to form, I had coiled myself up into the foetal position and was weeping convulsions. Again, not unlike the sound-healing class back in Bali. Which was very nice, because crying is old emotion sneezing.

But the joy of catharsis was brought to an abrupt end when something got really badly stuck in my eye – not the all-perceiving third eye, but my actual physical eye. My sobbing face had been pressed hard into a tuft of grass that some bit of thing had dug itself so stubbornly into my left eyeball that over an hour later my eye was still swollen, reddened and closed. Catapulted I was from eternal ecstasy to doubled over an outdoor sink in intense bodily discomfort, cupping handfuls of dribbling water to dunk my stupid swollen eye into. I took the next session of group introspection off.

Eventually, I decided, 'Screw this,' and plucked the eyeball clean out of its socket with a 432 Hz tuning fork, and when we got to back to Valencia I had it replaced it with one of those new bionic ones. Reader Warning: that last sentence is untrue.

This out-of-bodyness has not happened in that way again since, but on that sunny December afternoon, consciousness ripened like an orange. To the point where there was a real shift. New muscle memory was formed, forged in the mines of Mount Moria, as experiential proof of how first and foremost, at my very, very, very baseline, I am space consciousness *before* form.

After that, my 'I', my typical sense of myself and the world beyond, moved further away from my form or any other, and more into the processes that govern the experiences of form. Above/below/inside the confined sensation of the body. I don't know if this spatialness dies or lives forever, beyond I make no claims, but that unbodying experience did make me look forward to death.

This was also the dawn of a new ability to create a different kind of out-of-body experience. Not like this one, where someone pulled an ejector cord and sent me flying out of my body, but instead one where (parts of) my body disappears altogether and stay gone, and I stay sitting where I am. After, say, fifteen to twenty minutes into a rich session of woolgathering, my hands disappear and are replaced by rich, euphoric emptiness. Later, it began to include my feet, and then most of my extremities.

This crystallised for me how reality at rest is a kind of compass. Which we can use to reorient ourselves when we feel a little lost and in need and don't know where to go. Deep, restful reality, without anything trying to hold on to it, is a tempo where the body is at its optimal contentment. And the compass 'arrow' of sorts, which indicates what direction to navigate, is the sensation of spaciousness. And the sensation to put at my back like a prevailing wind is the sensation of my body.

Reality, and our perception of it, is completely dependent on how 'movingness' we are in its presence.

Finding more spaciousness in the practice means tuning deeper in to this multilayered stillness, so that going forward, one becomes a real connoisseur of aliveness, with an appetite for tasting its endless flavours. And the body begins to resonate more naturally at its optimal frequency, consistently and down to a deeper level on its own.

Later that night, my sight having been finally restored, we all sat silently around the crackling fire. Gazing into the flames, under the huge roadmap of stars above, each of us had in our possession little totems we'd made. Mine was a pinecone that I'd slotted into an orange peel, so that only the pointy end could be seen peeping out, and then I'd used that stringy central bit of the inner peel as a little sticky-outy tongue. He was called the Toad of Jealousy. We each constructed little totems to represent something we no longer wanted, something that was not serving our lives at all well. And by casting the totem into the flames, we would be relinquishing ourselves of the unhelpful thing.

I'd chosen jealousy. And as each pilgrim threw their totems into the fire one by one, I secretly hoped they saw and admired my toad because I'd put a lot of effort into him and he looked really cool.

I had been feeling these intense spells of possessiveness over my love. My whole imagination would coarse with unpleasant and distrustful fantasies to do with her betraying my trust. And because it was such an overwhelmingly unpleasant emotion to endure, its knock-on effect was that I'd begun resenting her for being the 'cause' of it.

Since always, the part of life in which I surrendered most of my emotional free will, the part where my emotions seized the most dominion by far, was in love.

The first time I ever told a woman that I was in love with her, ten minutes later we were in a blazing row.

I was twenty-one-ish, and it was late in London town and we were swaying in each other's arms on the dancefloor of a dingy downstairs pub. My hands cupped her smiling, blushing cheeks, and as butterflies hopped and bounced off the lining of my stomach I groped around the back of my mouth to find the words, 'I . . . I have fallen madly in love with you. I love you.' And she smiled even more broadly and blushed even redder, and proclaimed that she was so happy to hear it because she had fallen in love with me, too. And we embraced. We fell together and felt the warmth of each other's foreheads, and the love exploding like fireworks out of our chests.

Next thing, I'm storming up the stairs out of the bar with steam coming out of my ears and marching down a narrow, darkened alleyway. And then I boot this big green glass bottle as hard as I can out of rage and it goes flying and smashes to smithereens all over a wall painted jet black. And the bouncer from the next bar along lets out an 'Oi!' and comes rushing after me so I legged it around the corner.

When she eventually found me, sitting huffing on a stoop, I was inconsolable. And she hadn't the foggiest what was wrong.

'How dare you', I accused, 'cross the line just like that right in front of me? After *just* telling me that you love me? What vulgar timing! You're clearly a nutcase and a liar.'

What had *really* happened was that we had all continued dancing and having a laugh, but in my scared, mistrustful brain, she had started dancing a little too close to a friend of ours for my comfort. And my heart, having just been relocated to my sleeve, jealously confirmation-biassed in the blanks.

And the anger that swept me away was drunkening, it was a kind of dopamine anger. It felt righteous and good, so of course I had every right to pursue/defend it. Every right to let fly. And there was a cruelty in it, a punitive element, a petty desire to punish the woman I loved back if she 'caused me' pain.

The next morning, I woke up feeling like absolute dogshit, curdling in shame with her sleeping softly next to me. I limped out of bed and found a nasty cut on the tip of my left big toe.

And rowing aside, left to my own devices, my whole life I have always been a terror for ruminating in love. Tug-o'-warring in my head from one extreme to the other. If things went through a bad spell of not feeling good between she and I, my will to keep it going dwindled and fell to pieces under the weight of all the ruminating.

It was smothered under the yearning to sabotage the relation-ship by leaving her once and for all, so I could finally be free of the burdensome weight of the relationship. I was bewildered by this potent sense of hopelessness which would arrive with great clarity and certainty. This yearning, characterised by an inability to see any possible positive outcome beyond the present misery.

I would endlessly plan how I was going to break it off with her, and obsess over the moment of perceived freedom when I'd have finally managed to get away and be on my own. And I'd curse my own cowardice and procrastination, for not having the courage to just march in there and tear off the Band-Aid by telling her that the relationship was over.

But then, time would inevitably pass, and we would talk things over and find some peace, and then my heart was exploding for her again, and all I wanted to do was to hold on to her forever.

And I was so relieved and exhilarated that we'd made up, and that the nagging needling of incessantly breaking up with her in my head had subsided, and we were firmly back in each others' good books, back in warm cuddly love curled up together on the couch.

And both of these wildly opposing states had the exact same levels of integrity. They both, when they were happening, felt equally the truth. The giddiness of looking forward to the day when it would all be over, and then the struggle to see how on Earth I could have betrayed my heart so blindly.

And this oscillation from one extreme to the other, this insane tug-o'-war, was really the thing I yearned to be free of, not her. My whole life has been this way.

The problem with playing host to this is that it is completely unsustainable. And the longer it went on, never capable of landing in that elusive middle ground that other couples seemed to demonstrate effortlessly, the less possible it became to enjoy even the good times when they returned. Because the good times started coming with the sad knowing that they would inevitably turn back into more bad times. The bad times bled into the good times like ink. Like a desert island with coconut trees and an oasis being engulfed by rising sea levels.

And these difficult emotions were not things I awarded acknowledgement or time to process; I did not possess the awareness to be able to be present enough with them to properly look.

They were wielded as strengths at work, and avoided as weaknesses at home. Weaknesses that had to be concealed by behaviour
intended to come across as strength.

They were like my unruly children hijacking the sitting room
and tantrumming in an explosion of toys, noise and drawing on
the walls in crayon. And I thought that my job as overseer was to
get mad and shout and scream back at them, and as such, they
remained out of my control.

Before finding the spaciousness awarded by practising meditation, when I wasn't performing, the descriptive language I used
when referring to my most difficult emotions was I 'dealt with'
them. Which straightaway lumbers them with a problematic connotation. And hints at the suggestion that my unwanted emotions
were really an enemy, not my ally. 'Dealing with' my emotions
meant having to tolerate their presence. To reluctantly negotiate
with them like we were in a never-ending divorce procedure.
This, as you'd imagine, broadcast a confusing signal to myself.

And there were other times, in love, when I'd lost control in
more subtle ways, to the point where I wasn't sure I even meant
what I was saying anymore. Words, forming some viewpoint or
other, would come tumbling out of my mouth, and my whole tone
would be about winning by defending them, even though I was also
partly aware that what I was saying had little foundation. And the
deeper I dug myself into a hole, the more difficult it became to
renege and apologise. And then, a terrible nauseating moral challenge would rise up in me like the beating of a war drum,
demanding I be a man and tell the truth about what I was actually
feeling, as opposed to carrying on the dog-and-pony show of argu-
ing some trivial decoy. And when I failed that challenge, which was
frequently, I hated myself for it. Nowhere did I dislike myself more,
at times, than the self I found mirrored back at me in a relationship.

Or even more subtle than that, another thing I noticed was that, in love, whenever things were sunny and great and we were in a good mood, I would involuntarily sing little light-hearted tunes or make cute sighing noises just to fill any stretches of silence. And once I examined this habit under the light of awareness, I noticed that the real reason I was doing it was to subtly broadcast: 'I am in a good mood. Definitely not in a *bad* mood. Look at us! We are not fighting, definitely *not* fighting.' The subtext of my sound-making was almost an anti-warning, which communicated: 'Everything is fine. Look – everything's OK . . .' But, just like what Lao Tzu was saying after taking that huge dump in the forest, my *pose* of cheerfulness had a way of suggesting its opposing sorrow.

My early twenties in London was a checkered time, with frequent drinking.

Then, in the mornings, my mood was not good.

Once I did a play, and on the first week of rehearsals I remember another actor swanning into the rehearsal room all smiles and hugs and laughter, and I felt annoyed by it. I felt repelled by how cheerful and pleasant they were being.

I also remember that first Monday morning when we, the whole cast and crew, were due to assemble for the inaugural table read, and I overslept by two hours because I'd been out the night before butchering 'Lovin' You' by Minnie Riperton and other karaoke hits in a dingy dive bar until three in the morning.

I woke up that morning to the sound of my phone ringing and it said 'Elaine Stage Manager' on it. And a pal of mine sprang awake beside me, gasping in a panic, hissing, 'Just don't answer it, don't answer it!'

When London Underground finally did deliver me to the theatre, the director, Jim, took me aside into a little glass office and proceeded to scream in my face at the top of his lungs. I'll never forget the veins bulging red in the whites of his eyes. He was teetering treacherously on the threshold of firing me, with such statements as, 'By rights I should fire you', and, 'I would be well within my rights now to fire you', and, 'Typically, on a job of this scale, this qualifies as an *instant* firing', etc.

Fortunately, the thunderstorm subsided just before tearing that final layer of skin off my teeth, and I somehow remained employed.

The years rolled on as they insist on doing, and I ploughed on ever forward as a means of hiding from myself. And there were plenty of places to hide, like in the mirror at work, or in front of a screen, or under a woman's bed, or in the storage boxes in the attic of my homeplace, or in the garish spotlight of fame, and the rest . . .

I hid from my most painful emotions for so long that, like any neglected potato, I'd begun to grow weird legs.

> 'The most common form of despair is not being who you are.'
>
> Søren Kierkegaard

Ram Dass, whose book *Remember, Be Here Now* I read during the retreat, wrote 'The truth gets you high.' I can relate to this since, like him, my meditation journey was also preceded by plenty of recreational substance abuse. Like in Confession, the catharsis of alleviating his mind of some core truths he'd been holding back on left Ram Dass in a state of exhilaration, comparable to the feeling he'd only formerly felt while on drugs.

It's funny, it had been ages since I'd looked directly at my own lies. Hoping they would just drift away like rotting logs out to sea.

But, as a direct result of being ignored, just like the monkey mind, they'd begun to grow in size and influence. Until they began to embody me in the form of jealousy.

Before the five days of silence on the retreat, I genuinely hadn't put two and two together. I could not see the relationship between my unwelcome feelings of mistrust and my own mistrustful actions. I had not the eyes to see! That the latter was actually causing the former – not her and not anyone else. I was, once again, the cause of my own suffering. Executioner and condemned, all rolled into one.

So, after our retreat ended, I made my first real holy Confession. I said out loud all of the truths that I'd been holding back on. Every last thing that I felt compelled not to say to her, I reinterpreted as an invitation to say them.

Practising meditation gave me eyes to look directly into the sun. It made me see how my whole adult life I had denied giving love a real chance. I'd always assumed being free meant always keeping a little bit back for myself, but Ram Dass was right: it is in fact the exact opposite that is true. And it was only after sharing every last piece of myself with another person, especially the parts that were the most difficult, that a far stronger sensation of freedom emerged. A lightness of being unmatched by any drug.

· The Dream ·

We were way higher up than you'd previously said,

The pressure was clogging the back of my head.

Loud bubbles formed in the back of my brain,

When you caught my legs tense every time you changed lane.

We drove mired and gagged in a silence-sparked tryst,

For you keeping old Kleenexes stuck up your wrist.

You stuff these grim Kleenexes up in the cuff

Of that old fraying jumper where the wool is all rough.

And I hate when you hold me while wearing that thing,

And how wearing it brings on the spells of crying,

How the weave is all sodden with heavy feeling,

Those cuffs that could do with a serious wring,

To purge sodden snot from that old woollen weave.

If I saw it unravel I'd likely not grieve.

Inside the dust-blighted car window pane,

Daydreaming old pictures and fantasy rain,

Wondering if this pressure could damage my brain.

Before discovering meaningful meditation, before the age of thirty-ish, I engaged with creativity far less. 'Creativity' meaning doing creative things just for the sake of it. Because engaging with it, just for its own sake, made me feel a bit embarassed. And also, quite literally weak. The idea for a character would walk through me, or I would write something out in a flurry of flow, like some-one furiously rowing a boat out to sea, but far too soon I'd be physically and mentally spent. I did not possess the mental strength to sustain the state of flow, and so my typical mind resisted creativity.

A vital development as a result of developing a meditation practice was that it strengthened my mind enough to sustain the state of creative flow for longer, and awareness enough to realise the silliness of feeling embarrassed about it. And not just sustain flow for longer, but also allow the door to remain wider ajar through which flow could flow, so that ideas more frequently flowed in.

Then, after about three or four years, especially during times when I was spending many hours connected to the allsource, the influx of ideas, all lacquered with the sweet honey of possibility, became so prevalent that it became problematic. It became too much, in that it began to feel like an oversaturation. A different kind of tiredness/weakness came over me from an overexposure to creativity.

Then, a conscious step back from rich emptiness and forward into the material world became necessary again to re-establish a peaceful balance. But the key thing that going too far the other way taught me was that whatever in the world happens, there will never be a shortage of creative ideas if I want there to be, because I have direct access to the source of all creativity. For free, at home, whenever I want. I can direct consciousness to a state of being which allows for the imagination to go on a long *dérive*. And this simple seed of knowing, rooted in the earth of experience, evolved to become a great big Californian redwood of personal happiness and confidence. It was like discovering a kind of safety net stretching out beneath the tightrope of life, which meant that no matter if I did 'fall off' occasionally, things would still be absolutely fine. Without this, I believe I might have carried on living a fairly secure life, sure, but one that was about the continual unconscious pursuit of that safety net sensation in sources outside of myself. Which is a fool's errand, unfortunately – or maybe not a fool's but a child's. Such a life leaves one stranded in childhood until death.

Death retrieves the living like a friend who's been away.

His cries fell on deaf ears when he tried to make us stay.

He found a note but with no name explaining our away

To passing lands spun tight with

plans to muddy Death's foyer, but . . .

The silver hour holds lateness in the highest of disdain,

Objects with guttural grunting to

being a single second late.

So as Death retrieves what's left of us

at the platform of the train,

He throws his cloak around our backs

to keep our chills at bay

And guides us once upon a time

when we were suckling babes,

D'crying the peaceful womb where we'd

much rather have remained.

So, this has been my meditation pitch to you. To embrace your roots so the branches and leaves can look after themselves. I tried my hardest.

And as they say in show business, always end on a high note, so what better way than a few parting thoughts on death. As far as I can work out, the story of life goes from wanting, to wanting less wanting, to ultimately wanting less.

I plan on having a deathbed in a forest among lots of people who have bought tickets. There is a stage with some modest pyrotechnics, just a few fiery torches, and there are dancing musicians, dressed in costumes from the Middle Ages right up to the whatever Ages I die in. And they crowdsurf me down a procession and lay me into a coffin that is made out of sourdough. So that just in case I'm not fully dead I can still eat my way out.

And as the last of the energy leaves my body and converts itself into something else, my death audience leap up and down, throwing their arms in the air to encourage me up into the canopy of the trees. That's as now, but maybe when/if I get older, I'll want for a more modest affair. Like lying in a simple bed with clean white sheets, sun shining and birds singing outside the open window, surrounded by only twenty or thirty ticket-holders.

And when it happens, I hope to god my life doesn't flash before my eyes. That the process of death should have to include some kind of tedious retrospective.

Flashing Life S(l)ideshow.

☆ A doctor wiping me clean of placenta (and that's when I'm thirty!).

☆ Sitting crying on my mother's lap in her mother's sitting room, next to a chicken corpse on an Aga which had been stripped to the bone.

☆ Hocking up contributions to a giant spit pool with a bunch of the lads behind the labs, and then getting caught by Mr Murray and given four pages each as punishment.

☆ Sitting by the sea in Galway city, with the shortness of breath and queasy stomach of love.

☆ Scraping gum off a cork sandal with a thai coin with purple iodine all over my hands.

☆ Drawing a monobrow on Darwin on a £10 note.

☆ My mother's laugh, where her eyes stream with tears and she presses a tissue over her mouth.

☆ Waking up having slept funny, and experiencing the sensation of zero power to move my right arm.

☆ Singing karaoke at The Dolphin at three o'clock in the morning.

☆ Hitting the snooze button and rolling over and going back to sleep.

☆ And finally, masturbating by using resistance bands to strap myself down to a rowdy washing machine: the event that brings about my death.

I can't help wondering if that's not an indicator of our nature. That as life ends, of course *The Me Show!* would be the last one I'd want to watch.

Maybe it's Death's distraction technique. She's so bored by the frantic hysteria of the recently deceased, so to get us onto the boat she waves a shiny mirror in front of us as we're herded down the jetty.

Perhaps the last of my body's energy field will split into different parts. Some will end up in the machinery they use to wash the sheets. Some ripples through the air and creates a barely perceptible billowing effect on an old spider's thread in the corner of the room.

Or it drifts downwards through the ground like dew, to re-await its turn to tend back towards complexity and become something alive again. It might take a year or a million, who knows. Or perhaps we are all both alive and dead at the exact same time, the way our whole universe flickers on and off. And once we pass, we pass instantly from formlessness back into form, in some form or other.

I imagine the sensation of passing away is a function that my body knows well how to do, like sneezing or passing wind. After all, my ancestors have been dying succesfully for millions of years. I imagine it will be like . . . have you ever had that experience where a feeling passes through you, and you can tell it's something you haven't felt in years and years? An old echo of something, a concept that no longer has any words attached to it, because it has laid dormant on the seabed of your consciousness for such a long time, and has not been buffeted to the surface since you can't remember when.

Lastly, I would like to share one final useful and interesting technique to explore, when ready, in meditation. A little visualisation experiment where, once the mind is nice and settled down, I envision the moment just before and then the moment just after my death. Usually in the vision, I am at home lying peacefully in bed. My wife has outlived me, of course, so she is there dutifully rubbing my brow as others drift in and out of the room. The mood is not solemn: all the best funerals I've been to have always been the ones where the alive people are having a proper laugh.

I imagine my diminished, soon-to-be dead body from just above itself. It is tucked under a white sheet with only my face showing. Outside our bedroom window, the birds are chirruping and it's mid-morning. I want to fall asleep, but I exert effort to stay awake. To remain there a while for everyone else, for I know if I fall asleep now I won't wake.

Then, death silently approaches from below, with every shortening breath until my final one. And once the long rattly exhale of it is complete, I am no longer alive.

And then . . .

In a way, this meditation is almost like actually living through the final moments of my life. Call it a rehearsal. Call it playing dead. But the most humbling impression this technique leaves is of the inevitable moment just after, where life carries right on, business as usual. Which serves as an effective reminder of how unbothered reality is by my little passing.

I am looking forward to (a peaceful) death. Ask me again when I'm staring down the barrel of it.

Because, through practising stillness in meditation, it has become clear to me that the intention of the great intelligence, the same one that knits my skin back together if I nick it chopping garlic, the same one that grew my body from an egg and a sperm into the unknowably complex thing it is now, is to nurture and uphold my life, not to make it suffer.

THE PRESENT

Resources

Page numbers refer to page within Playing Dead*

p. 1   Itzhak Bentov, A *Brief Tour of Higher Consciousness: A Cosmic Book on the Mechanics of Creation*, Inner Traditions Bear & Co, 2000.

p. 7   Bill Burr, 'I used to think I was really driven, and now I realise I just can't bear to be alone with my thoughts.' https://podcasts.apple.com/gb/podcast/monday-morning-podcast/id480486345.

p. 10   Thomas Merton – www.thomasmertonsociety.org.uk.

p. 16   Dermot Healy, A *Goat's Song*, Faber & Faber, 1994.

p. 27   Caroline Di Bernardi Luft, Ioanna Zioga, Michael J. Banissy & Joydeep Bhattacharya, 'Relaxing Learned Constraints through Cathodal tDCS on the Left Dorsolateral Prefrontal Cortex', published in *Nature*, June 2017.

p. 28   Dr David Spiegel – *Healing the Mind with the Science of Hypnosis*, www.youtube.com/watch?v=k4xqcIzFWL8.

p. 28   James Joyce, 'A Painful Case', from *Dubliners*, 1914.

p. 28   René Descartes, *Discourse on the Method*, 1637.

p. 30   Deepak Chopra, 'I am, therefore I think': www.deepakchopra.com/about.

p. 30   The Earth Locker – *'Mind over Matter' with Deepak Chopra*, www.youtube.com/watch?v=ueEp6i9MDQk; https://chartable.com/podcasts/the-earth-locker/episodes.

p. 46   Osho – https://www.osho.com.

p. 50   Lao Tzu, *Tao Te Ching (Dao De Jing)*, 4th Century BC.

p. 60   Ram Dass, *Remember, Be Here Now*, Crown, 1971.

p. 90   Wim Hof: 'where focus goes, blood flows' – www.wimhofmethod.com/practice-the-method.

p. 91   Joe Dispenza, https://drjoedispenza.com.

p. 101, 102 Alan Watts – https://alanwatts.org/life-of-alan-watts.

p. 109 Quote from the epigraph to ANSWERED PRAYERS (1986) by Truman Capote, attributed to Saint Teresa of Avila.

p. 116 Quentin Crisp, *Manners from Heaven: A Divine Guide to Good Behaviour*, Flamingo, 1985.

p.131   Bruce Lee, 'Be water, my friend': from an episode of *Longstreet* called 'The Way of The Intercepting Fist'.

p.172   Samuel Beckett, *Endgame*, 1956.

p.174   Mooji – https://mooji.org.

p. 176   Samuel Beckett *Molloy*, Grove Press 1951.

p. 178   Manchán Magan – https://www.manchan.com.

p. 189   Samuel Beckett, *Waiting for Godot* 1953.

p. 196   Carlo Rovelli, *Helgoland*, Allen Lane, 2021.

p. 199   Kendra Cherry, https://www.verywellmind.com/implicit-and-explicit-memory-2795346.

p. 201   www.encyclopedia.com/science/encyclopedias-almanacs-transcripts-and-maps/planck-scale.

p. 202   Alexandra David-Neeland & Lama Yongden, *The Secret Oral Teachings in Tibetan Buddhist Sects*, Must Have Books, 2021.

p. 203   Itzhak Bentov, *Stalking the Wild Pendulum: On the Mechanics of Consciousness*, Destiny Books, 1988.

p. 207   Rebecca Solnit, *Wanderlust: A History of Walking*, Penguin Books, 2001.

p. 207   Nietzsche – www.themarginalian.org/2021/12/12/nietzsche-walking.

p. 212   Dr Qing Li, *Forest Bathing: How Trees Can Help You Find Health and Happiness*, Penguin Life 2018.

p. 218   Carl Sagan, *A Pale Blue Dot*: https://genius.com/Carl-sagan-a-pale-blue-dot-annotated.

p. 220   Akira Miyawaki: https://fellowsblog.ted.com/how-to-grow-a-forest-really-really-fast-d27df202ba09.

p. 240   Jordan Poppenk & Julie Tseng; 'Brain meta-state transitions demarcate thoughts across task contexts exposing the mental noise of trait neuroticism', in *Nature Communications*, 2020.

p. 243   Jack Kornfield, *The Wise Heart: A guide to the universal teachings of Buddhist psychology*, Bantam, 2009.

p. 249   Max Planck, *The Origin And Development Of The Quantum Theory*, Legare Street Press, 2022.

p. 251   G.D. Hatchard, A.J. Deans, K. Cavanaugh, and D.W. Orme-Johnson, 'The Maharishi effect: A model for social improvement. Time series analysis of a phase transition to reduced crime in Merseyside metropolitan area', Taylor & Francis online. See also https://research.miu.edu/maharishi-effect/, Maharishi International University.

p. 252   Maharishi Mahesh Yogi, Collective consciousness: https://research.miu.edu/maharishi-effect/theory-and-research-on-conflict-resolution.

p. 257   https://www.samharris.org/podcasts.

p. 258   Terence McKenna, https://www.organism.earth/library/document/birth-of-a-new-humanity.

p. 269   Søren Kierkegaard, https://academyofideas.com/2020/10/soren-kierkegaard-value-of-despair.

p. 269   Ram Dass *Love, Power, and Truth* 'https://www.youtube.com/watch?v=zxwjp5kBAZs.

Acknowledgements

Thanks to Rider, for giving me all the support and giving me far more time and space than we initially agreed.

Thanks to Augustina, for patiently listening to muddled bursts of many earlier drafts of this book.

Thanks to anyone who I shared stuff with and ye gave me a new perspective on it. I want you to know I stole all of your insights and peddled them as my own.

Lastly, thanks to the deep state attained through meditation – you playful, unfolding-in-dimension force, who used me as a keyboard tapper to write this book.